PREPARING TO SAY "I DO!"

Preparing To Say "I Do!"

HOW TO PREPARE FOR YOUR GODLY MARRIAGE (A BOOK FOR LADIES)

By Award-Winning Author,
Dr. Christine Topjian

Christine Topjian Publishing

Contents

Copyright vii
About the Author ix
The Idea For This Book xi
Dedications xiii
Other Books by the Author xv

1 Loving Yourself   1
2 You and God: A Starting Framework   19
3 How To Love Him When You May Not Yet Have
   Met Him Yet   38
4 Speak Life with the Power of the Tongue   42
5 The Company We Keep   50
6 When You Aren't Sure...Get Confirmation   63
7 Being Committed Before You Are Committed   72
8 So Blessed   82
9 How the Lord Speaks   96
10 Vision Boards   106
11 For Those Who Are Divorced or Husband(s)
   Deceased   113

12	Abuse	127
13	Divorce	135
14	Firmly Committed	143
15	Visualizing	156
16	That First Date	170
17	Now You Are Married....Now What?	175
18	Some Final Thoughts	180

Notes 187

Copyright

Published by Christine Topjian Publishing
(An Imprint of Authors Get Published)
www.AuthorsGetPublished.com

Toronto, ON

Copyright © 2022 by Dr. Christine Topjian

All rights reserved. No part of this publication may be reproduced, distributed, or transmitted in any form or by any means, including photocopying, recording, or other electronic or mechanical methods, without the prior written permission of the publisher, except in the case of brief quotations embodied in critical reviews and certain other noncommercial uses permitted by copyright law.

About the Author

Dr. Christine Topjian loves to help people along their journey to a stronger, deeper and more meaningful relationship with Christ. Having grown up a Christian but not fully understanding all that is available in Christ, Dr. Topjian wanted to create books and learning materials that would help readers of all ages and from all walks of life have and develop that meaningful relationship with Him (capital provided out of respect).

Her goal is to help you ensure that you are benefiting from this loving relationship and how to allow be open to the Holy Spirit's love and guidance.

Dr. Topjian wears many hats and loves to write on a variety of topics and in a variety of genres. Her Doctorate is in Prophetic Ministry from Christian Leadership University and her website is www.drchristinetopjian.com.

The Idea For This Book

The idea for this book came to me as I was actually completing another one. God put it on my heart to write this and if I know anything about God, it's that you need to follow through on step 1 before He shows you steps 2,3,4, and 5.

Marriage is an art. It is something we need to prepare for properly and we need to make sure that we are walking in with the right frame of mind. That's what this book does: it prepares you to enter into a Christ-centered marriage with the right frame of mind. Marriage (and all I know about it so far) is not something that happens by chance. It is something we have to work at, it is something we have to make a conscious choice to continue working at each day. Your husband will not be perfect and neither will you. And that's ok. Because marriage was created to be a union between an imperfect husband and an imperfect wife and with Christ at its center.

Why is God at the center? Because no human (no matter how much they try) can meet all of our needs and requirements. The only One meant to do that is God. In practical terms, you and your husband will have arguments, disagreements, difficult decisions to make and hard facts to face - how are you going to face all of those on your own? You were never supposed to. God is at the Center because He knew long ago that we were going to need Him and we were going to need to rely on His strength, His insight, His wisdom, His strategies, His kindness, and His forgiveness.

But that awesome marriage starts from when you are still single. When you are single, you have time to read, listen, prepare, spend time alone with God and mindfully prepare for what is coming. I know many women who enter into marriage thinking "it's going to be a big fairy tale and the guy will take care of me for everything!" Respectfully, it is not likely to be that way. Your husband-to-be is human just like you are and while it is a man's duty to take care of and to be there for his wife, he is going to need you to help him and take care of him too.

So, let's dive right in! In those sections where a reflection moment is provided (indicated by a lit light bulb), please do the reflection and answer the questions and what it is asking of you as honestly as possible. You will get so much more out of this resource if you do.

Dedications

This book is dedicated to every woman who desires to find, marry & stay happily married to God's chosen man for her life.

Blessings.

Other Books by the Author

"Check out the many books by Award-winning Author, Dr. Christine Topjian at DrChristineTopjian.com"

Other books by Dr. Christine Topjian (and counting):

Jesus Loves You

Love & Kindness

Give it to God

Hannah Can Read

It's in Transit

How to Be Led by the Holy Spirit

Are You Ready for God's Best for Your Life?

The Chrissie Series: Chrissie Meditates & Visualizes

Other Books by the Author

The Chrissie Series: Chrissie Goes Places

The Chrissie Series: Chrissie Prays

The Chrissie Series: Chrissie Speaks Nicely

The Power of the Give

God & Prosperity

Manifest It!

Manifest It ... Now!

Etes-vous prêts pour le meilleur de Dieu?

THE MONEY MANUAL

The Art of Getting It Done

Preparing to Say "I Do!" : How To Prepare For Your Godly Marriage (A Book for Ladies)

1

Loving Yourself

We have to love ourselves before we are going to love anyone else. I will repeat that because it is such an important point: we have to love ourselves before we are going to love anyone else. When we love ourselves, we look better, we feel better, we show ourselves kindness, caring and compassion and we make sure that we understand who we are in Christ.

Loving yourself means that you:

- treat yourself well
- love yourself
- speak kindly to yourself
- do kind things for yourself throughout the day
- dress well and in a way that makes you feel happy and respectful of yourself
- engage in wellness activities
- work out because you respect your body, your mind, your soul

- you surround yourself with people who love you and who will also treat you well
- you remove from your life people who do not treat you well
- you don't allow people to speak to you in a manner that is disrespectful
- you strive for achievements that you find meaningful
- you treat your family and friends with respect because you know they are important to you and are given to you by God
- allow yourself to make mistakes, realize the error, correct and move on

Not only are there so many ways we can show love to ourselves but we should be engaging in these acts every day. I know everyone has busy lives and many things they are doing. But we can take a moment and do something wonderful for ourselves. This is so necessary and we sometimes put ourselves on the back burner, as one to think of later. We have to value and love ourselves so that we can let others into our little worlds and accept their love for us as well.

I remember reading an article about a stunning young woman who was a model but because of her issues, she shared that she would regularly and deliberately work to injure herself and to hurt herself. She engaged in banging her head against walls, scraping and cutting herself, pulling her own hair out, consuming drugs and excessive alcohol, pushing away and eliminating people from her life that expressed a desire to help her, and wore clothes that were overly sexual because she shared that that was the only way she felt she had any value to anyone. I was shocked to read this because she was and is such a beautiful woman.

Reader, I don't know who you are or what you do but I have zero doubt that you also are a tremendously lovely and beautiful woman both inside and out. Are you treating yourself the way you deserve to be treated?

Our beauty comes from both within and our appearance.

Our beauty comes from both within and our appearance. It is really important to recognize and take note of our beauty and to love ourselves no matter what size we are, what color our hair is, what the color of our skin is, how we do our nails, do we have larger body parts or are they smaller? We need to learn to love ourselves tremendously and to treat ourselves tremendously well, regardless of how others may treat us, view us or speak to us.

 I'd like to take a moment here and ask you to take an inventory of your beautiful features. One of the biggest take-aways of this book is doing the exercises and putting into practice its teachings. You will get so much more out of this book if you put its teachings into practice and follow through, completing the exercises and answering everything honestly and completely.

So, back to the exercise: we are going to take note of your beautiful features, from your face to the bottoms of your feet. Let's look at each part and any defining features you may have, any special qualities or characteristics, if you have any beauty or birthmarks, if you are a more broad-shouldered female or a more petite one, the curvature of your eyebrows and if your eyes have a bit of a slant to them. Remember that God does not make mistakes when He created you and so you are so very beautiful just the way He made you. Include your specific details in the sections provided next to the items. The first section will deal with the outer (physical qualities) while the next section will deal with the inner (personality qualities):

Outer:
Hair: _____
Eyebrows: _____
Ears: _____
Nose: _____
Mouth: _____
Chin: _____
Lips: _____
Chin: _____
Neck: _____
Shoulders: _____
Chest: _____
Arms: _____
Collar bone: _____
Hands: _____
Nails: _____
Waist: _____
Pelvis: _____
Thigh: _____
Legs: _____
Knees: _____

Feet: _____
Toes: _____
Fingers: _____
Derriere: _____

Inner:
Sense of humor: _____
Kindness (to self and to others): _____
Intelligence: _____
Empathy: _____
Ability to relate: _____
Emotional intelligence: _____
Manner of speaking: _____
Sense of duty: _____
Ability to converse: _____
Ability to forgive: _____

- Something to make clear here is that you may not possess some of the physical items presented in the first section (ex. you may not have both arms or both legs, for instance), may I suggest jotting down in that section any advantages and benefits you feel have come from not having those parts. For example, a lovely and kind woman I know who has been in a wheelchair most of her life because of an accident when she was young and therefore has the use of only one of her legs said to me that she appreciates that she only has the use of one leg because it has shown her how to appreciate having that one leg and still being able to do so many of the physical sports that she still does. She said that having only one leg has made her a much more empathetic person to others and to understanding the plight of others. What a great way to view things! Good for her and good for all those who are fortunate to be around her and able to soak up her positivity!

The fact is, we can sometimes (or often) take our own physical and mental qualities for granted, saying "oh but everyone is like that". Not so. Not everyone is kind and nurturing and does good unto others. Don't take any of your qualities for granted. The right man will also not take any of your qualities for granted. He will appreciate everything you bring to the table and will appreciate you exactly as you are.

A woman I know was lovely and beautiful and kind and she was a bit overweight. As I saw her with the man she would later marry, I got to see how he saw her: as the most beautiful woman he had ever laid eyes on. Sure, he could have gone after a young woman who was as slim or fit as can be but when you heard the way he spoke about her and you saw the way he looked at her with such love, it was awe-inspiring. I asked him one time about something as simple as where to put down a bag of take-out we had all gotten together and she asked him to put it down on one of the folding chairs she had in her family room. She asked him to put it there "if he didn't mind" and if he didn't think it was too chintzy. His reply was "nope, I love it" and you could tell by the loving way that he said it that he really meant it. Even when referring to this little fold-out table, he was able to show her his love and appreciation for her because the fold-out table was hers and he was grateful to be able to be there to use it and he was grateful to be able to let her know that he was happy to use anything, so long as he got to be with her and around her. It was such a sweet moment.

My point in telling you this is that you may be a bit of a bigger girl or you may not have perfect eyesight, or you may not be in love with some of your features - please know how completely beautiful and wonderful you are and how much you should love all things about yourself.

Celebrate Yourself

We need to remember to celebrate ourselves a little (or a lot) every day. Doing wonderful things for us, taking care of our mental health and being good to ourselves. These things should be done daily. Regarding birthdays, some women can view their birthday as a sad day. "I am getting older", "I am no longer beautiful", "My biological clock is ticking", "I'm over the hill and no good anymore".

How about we stop that narrative!

Take the opportunity on each day to celebrate you, especially on your birthday and in the days leading up to your big day. Celebrate everything about you. Yes, we all have things we need to work on (we all do) but that should never stop you from celebrating who you are, where you are and all about you…positives and faults!

A woman once asked me "How do I stop hating some things about myself?" She was a woman who was struggling with her own sense of self and had had no relationship with God to speak of so she had never really learned to speak to herself or to view herself positively as the daughter of the most High God. I said to her that day what I am saying to you today: He made you perfectly, even with your "faults" and He loves you just the way you are. He cherishes your "imperfections" and wants you to know that He did not make any mistakes in creating you. Now, I also want to say here that no matter how hard we try or what we do, there will be some people who will not love you...and that's ok. More on that in the next section just below.

Not Everyone Will Love You...And That's OK

As wonderful as we all are and we are created by God as His perfect masterpiece, and we have everything to be grateful for no matter who we are, what we look like, the color of our hair, skin, body type, etc., the fact is that it is likely that not everyone is going to like or love you. That's just a fact of life and that's ok. We don't require everyone to love us in order to treat ourselves the way that we deserve to be treated and in order to view ourselves the way that we need to. Regardless of the naysayers, we need to respect and love our bodies, our minds, our sense of self, our abilities and all of our qualities. Our worth does not come from what others may say - it comes from our own inner appreciation and love for ourselves and from Christ's love for us. I will repeat this point because it is so very important for us to really internalize that last piece: Our worth does not come from what others may say - it comes from our own inner appreciation and love for ourselves and from Christ's love for us.

> We don't require everyone to love us in order to treat ourselves the way that we deserve to be treated and in order to view ourselves the way that we need to.

> Our worth does not come from what others may say - it comes from our own inner appreciation and love for ourselves and from Christ's love for us.

Now, we all have areas we need to work on and in order to do that, we need to identify which areas are the ones we need to work on. So, we are going to use a little exercise time here and I am going to ask you to self-inspect and to think about this a little bit: what are some items about myself that I need to lovingly and respectfully work on?

Please take a moment right now and jot down anything you need to write here. I also want to invite you to invite the Holy Spirit into this exercise and to see if He speaks to you about anything here. The Holy Spirit knows us perfectly and can help us identify (honestly and lovingly) the qualities and characteristics we need to work on. He can bring to our attention and our awareness the areas we need to work on and how we can improve. He can also help in actually improving our qualities. He is there for all of that!

_____

_____

People Can and Will Be Fickle

The fact is, people can be a bit judgmental and sometimes a bit fickle. They can treat you wonderfully today but tomorrow they can treat you like garbage. I have seen this happen and experienced this too. As such, we cannot rely on the opinions of others and how they view us to decide how we are going to view ourselves. Our self-concept has to be based on our own view of ourselves, on how Christ sees us, and not on every other person's view of us. Just because that co-worker or that team member or that acquaintance fails to see the beauty that is in us, it does not diminish our beauty and our awesomeness in any way.

These are things we sometimes tell younger girls and that is so important. But we need to remember that we, as older ladies, need and require just as much love, validation and reminders, and just as many reminders of our value and our worth as do younger girls. People are not going to start being great to you because they are older or because you are older. That is not reality. We have to have a strong concept of self in order to maintain a positive self-image because our self-image is going to dictate and influence all of the decisions and choices we make.

It will influence:

- how we choose to speak to ourselves
- who we choose to let into our lives
- who we choose to get advice from
- the quality of our everyday lives
- how we choose to let people talk to us
- our jobs or careers
- our husband
- the choice of words we use
- how we view the world around us and therefore, how we respond to it
- how we choose to teach our (future) kids to love themselves and to respect themselves

When we have a poor sense of self, that will likely create a bit of anger in us. We will tend to slump our shoulders, not likely look people in the eye when we are speaking to them, not respond in a loving and supportive way if and when someone makes a mistake (in general or toward us), etc. That anger or those feelings of less-than will manifest itself or themselves into our engaging in more conflict and strife in our lives, can undermine our sense of self worth even further, and will likely affect how we deal with everything going forward in life. When we have a poor sense of self, we are less likely to strive for greater career or personal aspirations, and the list goes on.

A lovely lady I will name Phyllis had aspirations for a loving home with a loving husband, wonderful, healthy and happy children, and a great career as a lawyer and litigator. But all through her life, she had heard "you are a loser", "you will never amount to anything", "you are a waste of life and a waste of space". This was repeated to Phyllis so frequently that she had virtually given up on a better life for herself. She had come from a family that was extremely poor, a father who drank away any family income that miraculously came in, a mother who would berate her and did illegal drugs and she was consistently mistreated by any boy who would deign to look in her direction. Phyllis was a lovely woman both inside and out but she didn't see herself that way and as such, her sense of self was terrible.

A friend of hers offered to take her to church one Sunday and reluctantly, Phyllis agreed. She had no way to get there and no appropriate clothes to wear so her friend agreed to give her some clothes and to drive her to church after they stopped by her house to help her clean up. Phyllis went to church and began to hear about and to listen to Jesus' love for her and the Father God's love for her. She was amazed that anyone loved her and that not only that, that someone as special as Jesus had died to give her life.

Phyllis was beginning to peel back the layers and the years of abuse and very poor role models that she had been subjected to and was just now beginning to see herself in a more positive way, a way that was the truth and that would begin to serve her wonderfully. Phyllis completed high school using the computer at the local library, began to read for pleasure and for school and learned about the power of the imagination. She moved out of her parents' trailer and into a home for girls so that the abuse would stop and she began to develop a sense of self esteem, allowing her to go out and befriend men who saw value in her and who would treat her the way she deserved to be treated.

When our sense of self changes, we begin to make changes about the kinds of people we will allow into our lives and certainly, into our spheres of influence.

Donna was a sweet and kind woman whose parents and friends built her up regularly. But she was always so down on herself. She had lovely red hair and lovely reddish features but because some people did not value that and used to call her "ginger", she had a very poor sense of self. I noticed this and talked to her about it and she tearfully explained how she had been mocked all her life for her red features, her blond eyebrows, her pale skin and more. I explained to Donna that she needed to start seeing herself the way that God saw her: as a beautiful masterpiece that He had created, giving her breath and life and putting so much goodness into her. This was a regular practice that Donna needed to engage in, working on it and reminding herself of her awesome qualities each day. When I met her, she was a young adult with very low self esteem. Because of the affirmations and positive words she would use, she grew to become a very confident adult who met and married a man who not only appreciated those features, but said they were some of his favorite qualities of hers. The right man for you will cherish your mental and physical qualities, just as you are.

Just as in the examples of Phyllis and Donna, you too may have people in your midst who are less than respectful of you, who put you down, who make you feel like less-than and who are not in the practice of making you feel good or lifting you up. These are people whom I encourage you to pray about whether to keep them in your life or whether you can move away from them.

Reflection: Are there any people you feel have not been positive in your sphere of influence and therefore, that the Holy Spirit may be encouraging you to remove (even temporarily) from your life? Write down your thoughts, ideas and reflections here:

_____
_____
_____
_____
_____
_____
_____

People Who Choose You....Do You Choose Them?

I remember very clearly a friend that I had who was about to get married. She and her husband had invited me to their wedding and were openly discussing with me whom they knew they wanted to keep in their lives as a married couple, and who wouldn't be kept. They had both clearly indicated to me that they intended to keep me "in". I reflected for quite some time about this and I remembered how this friend had a history of putting me down, throwing unfair comments in my direction and even questioning my Christian faith and how I applied my faith. I wondered if I was being too harsh and prayed deeply about this friendship. I felt that her husband-to-be was very kind and very genuine - he had always been such a kind gentleman to me but the Spirit was bringing to mind various instances and situations where she made it a point and a habit to put me down.

The Spirit reminded me that friends are supposed to make you feel good, to lift you up, to hear you out and not to judge you. The Spirit reminded me of other comments she had made in the past that unfortunately indicated some jealousy on her part (even though she was doing wonderfully in her life and was very blessed) and how she would try to justify why her worth to me (I never felt that she needed to justify this to me, ever). The Spirit provided a word of wisdom to me and a note of caution that she would not stop putting me down and that I needed to be more mindful in selecting my friends and my sphere of influence. The breaking point came when I had indicated to her a plan I knew was from the Lord for my life and she shot that plan down vehemently and quickly. I have enough experience to know that those who shoot down God's plans for your life are not going to be people you want to keep around very much.

> We must include in our lives people who build us up (even if that means telling us something that may be hard to hear) and certainly, ones who affirm our relationship with God.

Re-evaluating your circle is never an easy thing to do, in my opinion, but it is something you owe your future self the respect and the time to consider carefully. We must include in our lives people who build us up (even if that means telling us something that may be hard to hear) and certainly, ones who affirm our relationship with God and the things He is guiding us to.

Daniella was a kind and sweet lady who wanted the best for everyone. She was a skilled mathematician and also had an artistic side that enjoyed making pottery. Daniella had had the same friend since childhood, Ross. Ross had made many unkind comments to Daniella as they were growing and even one time joined in when a bunch of boys in their class began calling Daniella fat. When Daniella confronted Ross about this, he chalked it off to "they were just being funny" and left it at that. He knew it had been hurtful to Daniella. Now they were adults and whenever Daniella would have a date or a new prospect in her life, Ross would jokingly mock it and tell her that he would dump her as soon as he saw her. Daniella landed in counseling as a way of dealing with her issues of lack of self esteem. The counselor pointed out to her that Ross' incessant and unkind words (that he claimed were jokes) had taken a huge toll on her and that he was part of the reason she was suffering from such low self-esteem. The counselor encouraged Daniella to confront Ross about it and to advise him that she wished for him to stop doing that. She did and Ross' response was "you're such good ammo for this…why would I stop?" Daniella realized that by allowing this treatment to continue, that she was not respecting herself or valuing herself, and that at this point, it was her moment to make a call that was going to positively change her life and better reflect the new way she wanted to view herself and to be treated. Daniella made the decision to cut Ross off and to continue life without him.

As the months wore on, Daniella began to feel better, more cheerful, have a much greater sense of self and a man she had previously dated asked her out again. Daniella took action on making a move that would indicate her own self respect and that would serve her future well.

> How we see ourselves will manifest into the lifestyle choices, choices of friends, career choices and much more that we will undertake. Make sure you are making good, emboldened and powerful choices for your life.

How we see ourselves will manifest into the lifestyle choices, choices of friends, career choices and much more that we will undertake. Make sure you are making good, emboldened and powerful choices for your life. And the best way to do that is simply by asking the Holy Spirit to show you who is who in your life and how you should proceed with them.

2

You and God: A Starting Framework

Foundations: The basis to finding your God-given spouse is your own relationship with Christ. You cannot find him without Him. Said differently, you need to develop your own relationship with God, hearing from the Holy Spirit, in order to find him and to know that this is the one meant for you.

Many people today flock to online websites to find their mate, not giving much or any thought to where God leads you to find your person. Also, don't forget that it's not just a matter of finding him - you have to recognize that he is the one, you have to meet him, talk to him, build that relationship with him and actually get married, and the fun doesn't end there. After you actually get married, you then have to stay happily married. This is where I have seen many couples who were meant to be get derailed.

A woman I know who had some faith but never really spent time with God talking about her husband, developing that close relationship with God and with the Holy Spirit, did in fact get married and began a lovely marriage journey with her husband. Until she discovered he wasn't perfect. He would do this and that or this, that and the other and it would get on her nerves. Despite my encouraging words to talk to him about things, to work on things with him and to pray for and with him, she instead chose to just opt out of the marriage. My point is that we have to have that close relationship with God in order to get to (and successfully complete) every single stage of this process.

Marriage was always meant to be between 1 man and 1 woman and God. We were never supposed to do this "marriage thing" on our own or in our own strength. Never. Because we are imperfect people so without God's help, insight, provisions and strength, we are not going to be very successful at marriage.

That's why this book starts by talking to you, the woman, about your relationship with God through the indwelling Holy Spirit. It is very important for men to also have this relationship with God through the indwelling Holy Spirit but this book focuses on the female. Therefore, one of the goals of this book and this program is to help you put in place those healthy Spirit-filled habits so you can have the best chances at successfully navigating your relationship with your future husband when the Lord chooses to bring him along to you, from beginning to end. No matter what stage of the journey to marriage you are currently in, it is so important to put these foundational practices into place from now. It takes time for foundational practices to be developed, honed and worked on. Also, what may take one person several months may take another a couple of years…you are on God's timeline and journey, not anyone else's.

So, how do we begin (or continue) cultivating that relationship with the Holy Spirit? Are there questions we need to ask from the Holy Spirit in order to know what to do, how to do them, and when to do them? What happens when we are feeling weak or we do not feel that we have the motivation to keep going? How do we handle naysayers who may not be on the same wavelength as us?

There are many things you can do to help yourself. In this book, I will guide you to developing that close relationship with God and the Holy Spirit and to let Him show you the best ways for you. I will also show you what it means to be mindful and to recognize when something is shifting in the right direction because without being mindful of this, we can easily miss it when it happens.

Here is a list of some things you can begin doing:

- Read Scripture and ask the Holy Spirit to speak to your heart about what you are reading, asking Him to illuminate certain passages that specifically apply to you and are relevant to you
- Pray for you and for him - you may not know who he is yet or you might but you haven't met yet or any variety in-between. Nonetheless, nothing stops you from praying for you both, for your union and for the strength and presence of mind of knowing it when it happens.
- Do not read secular books on finding your right man. God's ways are not those ways so you will be confusing yourself unnecessarily and causing yourself to move in the wrong direction.

- Spend time listening to Christian sermons. This is a phenomenal way of better understanding the ways of God and as such, you will be able to get a much better sense of how, when, where you are going to meet him.
- Stay open. He may not be, look like or act the way you think he will or should. Respectfully, you are not perfect either. You will both need to work on yourselves and there is nothing wrong with that.
- Learn to journal. Begin by writing out your thoughts, ideas and opinions and ask questions of the Holy Spirit through your journaling. For example: "Is there something specific I am supposed to be doing to help this along? Is there somewhere specific I am supposed to be going?" and then wait and listen for any responses and prompts.
- Ask the Holy Spirit to give you some visual images (this will be covered in much more depth later in the book) because knowing how to allow the Holy Spirit to visualize blessings God wants to bring you is essential.
- Remember to be grateful. Giving thanks for the blessings you already have helps bring in new blessings. This is extremely important because it helps us remember the good things God has already brought us. Bearing that in mind, we should have faith to know that He will bring us more good.

Developing Your Relationship With God

This is essential and non-negotiable. We have to develop an awesome, close relationship with God in order to get to know His ways and His communication. I liken this to having a best friend:

you know most (if not all) about your best friend and as such, you know what he or she is thinking, feeling, wondering before he or she ever has to say it. You know your best friend and their ways. This is no different. After all, how can we expect to have His best for our lives if we don't even know Him?

When He Tells You Who He Is

This is very cool. When God finally reveals to you who this man is, it's a really cool moment. It's like someone finally told you the most awesome secret and while you may not fully understand it yet, you can trust that this is the best bet for you. God created you both and knows you both. He knows how you both think, what dreams and desires He has put on both your hearts and He knows your good qualities and your faults. As such, He has matched the two of you up perfectly.

He may be someone you met at work, through friends, at a party, on the bus, in class, maybe your mom set you both up or you just happened to meet him "by chance". I can't tell you how many stories I have heard of how God brought two people together and how He worked on them both before He brought them together.

It Doesn't Mean He Is Ready. It Doesn't Mean You Are.

One of the hardest-learned lessons for me was when I realized that my guy was not yet ready for me. He had some things he needed to work through and despite not loving that fact, I simply had to accept it.

It also doesn't mean that you are ready for him and the level of relationship that will be required to make a marriage work. You may need some time to develop, just like he may too.

If this happens, I caution you to be kind and patient about it. I made the mistake of getting angry at that and to this day, I am sorry that I did. It was wrong of me to get mad at him for needing the time that he did to grow, develop, mature and be the person who was ready for that level of a commitment with me.

> You cannot move on and be fully committed to your husband when you are holding on to past romantic prospects.

Please understand that if God is making you wait, it is a really good opportunity for you to work on yourself. Working on yourself can mean taking some time to heal from past hurts, past disappointments, grow in your faith, take new classes, pick up a hobby, start something you find exciting and much more. For example, if you are having a hard time moving on from a past relationship that God has told you is not the right person, then using this time to move on from that would be very wise. You cannot move on and be fully committed to your husband when you are holding on to past romantic prospects. And this is an area where you need to be really honest with yourself and hold yourself to this because if you are not doing this part of the process, you will find things much more difficult and much more complicated later on. One of my favourite pastors, Chip Ingram said it perfectly: true love does not share. Your husband-to-be is not going to want to share you physically, mentally or emotionally with another and will expect that same consideration from you. When you are in agape love with someone, you do not want to share them with others. You want to build a covenant of exclusive love with that person.

We are all imperfect and we all need to work on ourselves in order to be the best possible version of ourselves.

During the waiting period (perhaps your man has told you that he isn't ready and that he needs some time for himself), pray for him. Pray for him to be well, to develop that closer relationship to God, for him to appreciate you more, for him to heal and to develop in a way that will make him a strong marriage partner for you and a great dad to yours and his kids, etc. Use the time wisely to pray for the both of you and for your lives together.

Many single women only use the time when they are apart from their future husbands to just wait without doing the work that is involved. They don't take the time to pray for situations to improve, for you or he to get better and healthier, they don't pray for a stronger relationship for themselves or their spouse. That is what I call wasting your waiting time. If God is asking you to wait, it is with good reason. He needs time and so do you and without you both taking that time, your relationship will not be as strong as it needs to be. When people do not get the time they need to grow, to develop, to heal, they begin to lash out at others and they become a different person. They become a harsh and angry person because they are not having their needs met.

Gratitude & Blessings Journal

It is very wise to keep a gratitude and blessings journal. A journal such as this will be a wonderful, daily reminder of the blessings you already have and how these have enriched your life and the lives of those around you. It would be great to include everything in this journal. Don't ever take any of your blessings for granted because as you may or may not realize, there are many out there who may not have those blessings and are praying for the very things you take for granted.

For example, a lady I know I will name Alma had a wonderful home life. She was blessed with a kind and loving husband who supported her in every way. She also had three wonderful, healthy and happy children who loved to spend time with mom when they were not reading on their own, playing with their tools or spending time with their friends. Alma lived in a beautiful home and was a stay-at-home mom, as her husband earned a very good living, so she did not have to work. Alma was also such a pretty woman and she had such a loving family and loving in-laws. She had an idyllic life but she did not appreciate it. She took it for granted and failed to treat her husband the way he deserved to be treated. She failed to treat her in-laws the way they deserved to be treated. She failed to be kind to the house help who were hired to make her home even more beautiful and even lovelier. Alma did not appreciate the blessings she had. She was also a fantastic painter who made beautiful works of art that would appear periodically in art galleries downtown and for which she was paid handsomely, when she decided to work on it. Alma had it all but did not appreciate it. Slowly and as each day wore on, she did not treat those around her the way they deserved to be treated. She pushed everyone away and never demonstrated gratitude for all her blessings. As time wore on, Alma lost each of her blessings.

We can be given the world but if we do not appreciate what we have, if we do not have that relationship with God reminding us of how good we have things and remembering how we are supposed to treat our spouse, people will only take so much for so long.

Take time each day (however you can) and write, draw, jot down notes, use your gratitude journal. We all have difficulties and challenges (that's a given) but if we take time to really stop and appreciate the good things we have, we will realize how very richly blessed we are.

You don't have to live in a huge home to be blessed.
You don't have to drive the most luxurious car to be happy.
You don't have to have 0 issues in your marriage for it to be ordained.
You don't have to experience 0 issues at work for your work life to be satisfying.

Tough Times. Great Realizations.

There will be times in your future marriage where there will be harsh waters & difficult situations and circumstances. Things will not be going well, the tide will be hard and things will not be jiving in the way that you would want them to. When those times come, it is really important to have that solid relationship with God already in-place so that you know how you are supposed to handle something. You may have said something that turned your mate off, you may have done something that he found to be inconsiderate, you may have reacted in a way that he found inappropriate. You will experience times when things are not going very well and you may not understand why. It is those times where you have to lean on God, on His wisdom, on His insights and on His ways. He will bring to your attention what you may have said or done wrong. He will bring to your mind the moment or the time when you said something your spouse did not appreciate and may have really hurt him. He will show you how to fix the situation because He knows you both better than you know yourselves. In those times, pray and listen carefully to the wisdom and the guidance.

When Roxanne was having a hard time in her marriage with Jed, she didn't know what the problem was. Roxanne was a fairly reflective person but she did not understand why Jed took what she said so badly. He hadn't spoken to her in three days and clearly needed his space to process and to heal. Roxanne realized that what she said or did had really hurt her husband so she began to pray about it, asking God to help her understand why her husband was so angry with her. He was not often in the habit of freezing her out. When she prayed, she realized that she had called him an unkind name to his face. She had actually forgotten that she had done so because it was in the heat of the moment but upon closer reflection, she realized that she had fully hurt her husband's feelings and in a way that was particularly damaging because he was freezing her out. While she understood now that her words were unkind, she still did not understand the freezing out part. So, she continued to pray for insight about that. The Lord spoke to her and revealed that in the past, Jed's stepmother had done the same thing but in very harsh ways, and these actions from his stepmother had done him much harm. His stepmother was almost verbally abusive to him in the way she used to do that and the only way his gentle self knew to cope with it was to freeze her out so that he could protect himself and heal. He was doing the same thing with Roxanne - it was a protective stance and it was the only way he knew how to cope. Roxanne did not know that about her husband so this was a major revelation to her.

As soon as Roxanne realized what she had done and the damage it caused, she went to her husband and apologized. She apologized deeply for using the words that she did and for making him feel the way he had been. She explained that as she reflected on her words and her actions, that the Holy Spirit had revealed to her that she was out of line and that that would not happen again - that she needed to find other, positive and relationship-building (not destroying) words to build him up and make her point, rather than tearing him down. Within a half day, Jed had time to process his wife's apology and he forgave her.

Tianna and her boyfriend were having a great time out with his family. It was her first time meeting them and while she was nervous, things could not have been going better. They were all getting along, they were laughing and making jokes, they were kindly asking her about herself and seemed to appreciate all her qualities. She was having a great time and her boyfriend seemed to be confirming that things were going really great. Until something happened and things went bad, really quickly. The mood had suddenly changed and Tianna had no idea why. All of a sudden everyone at the dinner table had gotten quiet and there seemed to be an uneasiness in the air. Had she said something? Had she done something wrong? She couldn't figure it out.

Tianna excused herself and went to the ladies room. There, she prayed for the Holy Spirit to reveal to her what had gone wrong.

Immediately, she remembered a comment that she had made and the Spirit brought to her attention that her boyfriend's family may have been laughing at the comment but if you observed more closely, they had been uneasy about her comment. Tianna asked God if He could help her by creating a situation where she could be alone with her boyfriend for a few minutes so that she could ask him about this. Sure enough, that opportunity came. Her boyfriend met her at the area where the ladies room was and they talked about what had happened. He explained that it was due to the comment she had made right before they sat for dinner. He pointed out that while there was nothing wrong with what she had said, that the family was very sensitive about the topic of the joke and they didn't feel they knew her well enough yet to tell her that it made them a little uneasy. Tianna apologized and her boyfriend said he would help ease the situation when they went back to the dinner table.

Without the insight from the Holy Spirit, Roxanne may not have realized this and it could have done irreparable damage to their marriage and the simple issue with one comment gone wrong may not have been brought to Tianna's attention without the Lord showing her what had actually happened.

He is there to guide us and to help us through each step.

Reflection time: Has there been a time when you have said something or done something to your guy that made him feel bad? Have you ever considered apologizing to him for that? Have you ever spent time making him feel loved, cherished, supported and even when changes were needed, have you brought those up in loving, supportive, relationship-affirming ways?

Have You Asked God What Marriage Is Supposed To Look Like?

Have you ever asked God what a Godly marriage is supposed to look like? Then, have you ever asked God what your marriage is supposed to look like? Marriage in God's way is often not explored or talked about much in our daily society. Instead, we see relationships that have nothing to do with God being formed, people marrying people at first sight, wife or husband swaps, broken homes, broken relationships, rampant misunderstandings, harsh words spoken, custody battles, aggressive behavior, contentious divorces and much more. None of this is ever how God intended marriages to be.

So, have you ever asked Him what marriage is supposed to look like? Have you ever asked Him how you are supposed to meet your man, in particular? Have you ever asked Him how the two of you are supposed to come into relationship with each other?

I remember over a decade ago (when I had no active relationship with God) and a "friend" (I use that term loosely) suggested I go online to meet my husband. She was not a Godly woman either so she certainly wasn't suggesting that because she had prayed about it for me. She just made her own suggestion. So, I went online to a website and met a man I thought was good looking and interesting. We did pursue a lengthy relationship - one that I came to regret significantly. I discovered in later years that this way and this relationship was never God's will for me and that I had gotten caught up in a wrong situation. I had not prayed about His will for me. I didn't even really know He had a will for me in this respect.

You need to be in active, effective relationship with Him in order to be guided and supported each step of the way.

 Reflection time: Do you see the importance of building (or continuing to build) your relationship with God? Do you see why it is important for you to spend time alone with God and develop your active relationship with Him so that you know how and what to do regarding your future spouse? Spend some time with Him today and ask Him what He wants to speak to you about in these regards. Remember to ask lots of questions, probe and when you are not sure about a point, ask about it. God loves to be asked many questions. Finished this section but then realized that you would like to ask more questions? Come back to this section and keep asking. No harm in that.

How To Hear From The Holy Spirit

In my book, The Art of Getting It Done, I go through a specific process one can begin to use to hear clearly from the Holy Spirit. It is a very simple process but one that will require some practice. I will include that same process here:

Step 1 - Sit in a comfortable space with no distractions (or the least number of distractions)
Step 2 - Tune in to the Lord and ask Him in your mind to speak to you
Step 3 - Pay attention to any words, thoughts, and images that come spontaneously into your mind
Step 4 - Tune in carefully to see the words, thoughts and images that come to your mind and look at them carefully. Like when you are looking with a magnifying glass, try to look at the details as carefully as possible
Step 5 - Write down / draw all that you see

They Charge For This. God Doesn't.

Something important to point out here is that there are many matchmaking companies out there - companies that will promise you that they will find you your ideal person, set things up for you both, and ensure that you are compatible in as many ways as possible.

Simply put: that is not God's way.

We have been given free will, therefore you can go about things that way but it would be unwise to do so. *God has that special man for you and isn't going to charge you to reveal him to you. All He is going to ask is that you be in an active, loving relationship with Him.*

You see, when we don't know God's ways, we can easily fall into unfortunate circumstances. We can easily fall into situations that are not only not meant for us, but that can, in the end, be quite dangerous for us. I don't know about you but marrying a man thinking he is the right person sounds pretty dangerous to me. So let's avoid all of that.

I remember when I had met my ex online. He seemed great and his profile intrigued me. A "friend" (using that term very loosely) suggested I go online to meet my guy and so I did. At the time, I had no relationship with God so this was a decision I was making purely on my own. I messaged him and we began to exchange messages. He seemed nice and cute and sweet and like a real family man. I found him tremendously attractive so I was looking forward to meeting him. I ended up dating that man for a couple of years and looking back, there were warning signs from God, red flags, and without the benefit of the knowledge from the Holy Spirit, I was completely on my own making all of these decisions. It was not a wise way to proceed because I am only human and cannot see the true nature of someone's heart. The Holy Spirit can and it is only by tapping into that and asking Him that we will get those answers.

Your Quiet, Special Place

It's important to have a special place where you can go, meditate and hear from God directly. If you live in a busy home and you are having a hard time finding a quiet space, think carefully about a quiet space you can access. You cannot hear clearly and accurately without a special, quiet place in which to be.

Also, one of the tools that I think is very helpful is the following: imagine yourself as a little child, sitting on Jesus' lap, being loved by Him and being cared for by Him. Remember that He is our go-to, our Helper, our Confidante - literally the One we can go to with all our problems and He will help us feel better *"Then you will experience God's peace, which exceeds anything we can understand. His peace will guard your hearts and minds as you live in Christ Jesus."* (Phillipians 4:7)

So choose your quiet space where you would like to meet with Him and spend some time there. Imagine yourself as a little girl sitting with Jesus, telling Him your thoughts, problems, ideas, etc. This time with Him can and should feel like a vacation because that's what life with Jesus should be like - a little vacation where we know that in this partnership, He is taking care of your worries, your troubles, your concerns, etc.

When you are in this special time and you are spending time with Him, asking Him many questions would be really helpful, such as

"Where am I going to meet him?"
"When should I go there?"

"What should I know about him?"
"Does he know about me?"
"Is he praying for me?"
"What should I be praying for him?"
"What can You tell me about him?"

The Lord is looking to answer these questions for you, He wants to bless you with this man, so you asking these questions is never a problem. It is actually good and proactive. One of the things I want to make really clear here is that you can be at any point in the process and still ask probing questions. In other words, you can not know who he is yet and you can ask these questions, you can know who he is because the Holy Spirit has already spoken to you about him and you can still ask this questions, you can know where you are supposed to meet him because the Holy Spirit revealed it to you and you are looking for more information about it. At any stage, you can ask, ask, ask and probe, probe, probe and then listen carefully of course.

Use the Term "My Husband" If You Are Not Sure

If you are not sure who he is yet because the Spirit has not revealed it to you, then simply ask these questions with "my husband" instead of his name. This will help ensure that you are asking in a general nature so you are not asking for the wrong person.

3

How To Love Him When You May Not Yet Have Met Him Yet

Simply put: you don't have to have met your future husband yet to love him. You can do all of the following for him even before even knowing his name:

- Pray for him
- Pray for his family (your future in-laws), and his loved ones
- Pray for God to speak to his heart and to let him know you're "out there" praying for him
- Pray for his protection and safety
- Thank God for him (creating him, and marking him as your husband)
- Ask the Lord to help him find his way

- Ask the Lord to tell you all that He can about him (his ideas, his hopes, his dreams, etc.)
- Add his name into your gratitude journal
- Put him and your prayers for him up on your vision board (more on this in a later chapter)

One of my favorite things to do before I even knew the name of my husband is I used to pray for him, his needs and more. Here is what that prayer looked like:

Lord Jesus, I pray for You to help my husband through anything he may be going through right now. I pray for You to help him find his way and for You to bless him. He has hopes and dreams that I don't know about yet and I am asking You to help him work through all that he needs, so that he can be the man You and he desire for him to be. In Jesus' name. Amen

He Will Tell You Who He Is

God likes to surprise but He is looking to reveal to you who your future husband is. Remember that He wants to bring this man to you in matrimony, even if He has not yet. So when you ask, know and be confident that He will tell you. It may take some time but He will reveal who he is to you.

When He tells you to do something or to go somewhere: when you get a feeling or an idea that you are supposed to go somewhere or do something, do not tarry. Go, do. Because that is His way of leading you and guiding you. If you don't go, you could miss out on a divine meeting and Him trying to answer your prayers. I want to make it very clear how important it is to listen to and to follow through on any prompts He gives you.

A woman I will name Melissa had been praying for months for her future husband. She did not know anything about him but she had a pretty close relationship with God and so she felt confident that while He had not yet spoken to her to reveal his name, identity or where and when she would meet him, she felt very confident that He would reveal this to her in time. One day, she received an invitation to a party that was completely unexpected and she didn't even know the people who were throwing the party but she felt quite sure that she was supposed to go to this party. She felt quite confident that she was supposed to go to this party because he was going to be there. She had already made plans for that day and so she prayed about whether she should go to the party or to her plans. The Lord could not have been more clear in telling her that she needed to be at the party, despite the fact that she already had plans and that she did not know anyone who would be at the party. So, she followed through and went with a friend of hers who had told her about the party to begin with. At the party, she was introduced to a very nice man who was shorter than her and younger than her. There didn't seem to be anything particularly striking or stand-out about him but someone there introduced him as Roger. He was a mechanic who lived and worked in the same city as Melissa, but she had never actually met him. Melissa did not sense anything specific about Roger so she excused herself and went to the powder room. She prayed about this Roger man and asked the Lord if he was her future husband. The Lord asked Melissa to be patient and go back into the party. She did. Melissa chatted with Roger, they joked about his career and hers, and they talked at-length about all things faith-based. Roger then said "Melissa, you should meet my brother,

Ryan. I think you two would really hit it off." In her soul, Melissa felt like a jackpot just went off. At the sound of Ryan's name, Melissa got giddy-excited and couldn't wait to meet and chat with Ryan. Roger invited Melissa to a BBQ he and his friends would be throwing that weekend. Melissa graciously accepted and there, she met Ryan, the man who would be her husband and father to their children. It took a few steps to get Melissa to where she needed to be but in fact, He got her there. It took listening, obeying and being patient to the prompts.

Putting It Out There, In Faith

When you don't yet know who he is, put it out there in prayers and in general terms. Tell God that you recognize that He obviously knows who he is and everything about him, so you can let Him know that you are relying on Him completely and that you are putting your faith and trust in Him, that He will bring you your husband and that all you ask is for God to prompt you if there is something in specific you need to do to help this along. Remember, God loves when we rely on Him and when we tell Him that we are relying on Him.

I remember when a friend of mine and I did this. It was so simple. We sat in my car with our sodas in hand and we looked up to the sky (yes, in the car) and we told God that we are both His children and that we are both relying on Him and trusting Him!

4

Speak Life with the Power of the Tongue

> The tongue can bring death or life; those who love to talk will reap the consequences. (Proverbs 18:21)

Just as it says in Scripture, life and death are found in the power of the tongue. When you speak positive, life-affirming words, you will get positive circumstances and the reverse is also true. Now, this is not to say that when you speak positively, challenges will not come. That they will. But you will be speaking positive words and you will be encouraging and calling forth good things into your life.

This context is no different.

If you are speaking negatively, it is really important to change your words to positive ones. If you are speaking words such as "I will never meet my future husband. God doesn't care about me. He has forgotten me", then you will be reaping negative into your life.

If you are one who has been speaking negatively for some time, it will take time to get into this new habit. Just like the rudder of a ship changing course, it will take time for your life to go into a new, positive direction. We have to keep in mind that despite all that is going on around us, that we need to speak positive words over our lives. We cannot expect to speak negative words and then have and experience positive. It doesn't work like that and changing course can take some time so you will need to be patient.

We cannot speak negative words and then expect to have and to experience positive things. It doesn't work like that.

If You Are Not Saying Anything

Many people talk about speaking positive words and not negative ones. But how about if we don't say anything. Is that bad or good? It's bad. As humans, we naturally usually (there are always exceptions) have a tendency to speak or to view things negatively. When we don't say anything and we are neutral, we tend to move toward negative thoughts, which will eventually manifest themselves into negative expressions of those thoughts. So not saying anything will eventually turn into thinking and speaking negatively.

So instead, we need to ensure that we are speaking and saying and thinking positively. We may be having a bad day or we may be in a bad mood and we might immediately start speaking and thinking negatively. Catch yourself. Don't allow yourself to fall into that trap and to be speaking or thinking negatively. Remember that neutral means that you will soon move into negative so keep things positive as often as possible (yes, even if you have to force yourself).

Examples of Positive Phrases

I always find it helpful to provide examples to readers. Examples give you a more concrete understanding of the concept and help you contextualize things.

Here are some examples of positive words and then I will provide some positive words specifically for the context of meeting your future husband (note that all sentences are written in the present - when we are looking to have something, we always speak in the present to indicate that we know God is presently blessing us with it):

- I am a kind, loving woman
- I thoughtfully consider the feelings of others

- I speak thoughtfully all the time, factoring in how the other person may feel hearing my words
- I am kind to others
- I love myself
- I appreciate my body just as it is
- I have a sound mind
- People enjoy spending time with me
- I am grateful for each day, even if that day holds challenges
- I enjoy spending time by myself
- I am a person of value
- Jesus thinks I am to die for
- I appreciate every one of my blessings
- I have a beautiful mind
- I have a beautiful body
- I am praying for my husband and the Lord hears and answers all prayers
- The Lord is bringing me my husband, in a way that only the Lord can
- I rely on the goodness of God's character to bring me the right man
- I am meeting and coming together with the right man for me
- The prayers I am praying for my husband are so effective and are improving the life of my husband as I speak or as I think them
- The Lord is never late in bringing blessings to His children
- I am listening and paying attention carefully so that when the Lord brings me my husband, I will know through the Spirit, that it is him
- I am allowing God to work in me so that I am ready and prepared for when He brings him to me
- I am a kind, loving, blessed and patient wife

- I enjoy supporting my husband mentally, emotionally, psychologically, spiritually and intellectually
- I enjoy and regularly pray for God's best for my husband my in-laws
- I trust that the Lord is blessing my husband with the right people around him who will encourage him to doing God's best in his life and for our lives together
- I pray and trust that my husband is staying away from detrimental things such as drugs, alcohol and more. Please help him to do so, Lord.

Reflection time: Have you been thinking and speaking negatively? For how long have you been doing so? Are you ready and willing to change this course of previous action and change it so that the proverbial rudder can begin to go in the opposite direction? Write out your reflection here:

_____
_____
_____
_____
_____
_____
_____
_____
_____
_____

_____
_____

 In an attempt to begin changing course, I invite you to begin to write out 3 positive statements for your love life. Write out 3 positive statements that indicate that you will 1) have faith in God regarding your love life 2) you will commit to speaking (or continuing to speak) positively over your life 3) that you will commit to continue doing this (I encourage you to actually put in reminders in your journal or in your phone so that you can commit to and document your actions.)

_____
_____
_____
_____
_____
_____
_____
_____
_____
_____
_____
_____
_____
_____

___

Putting It Out There

The time prior to knowing who your future meant-for is can be challenging. Not knowing can, well, suck, but we have to keep in mind the power of putting it out there. Putting it out there is akin to putting positive thoughts and words out into the world and knowing that it will reap you a good and positive harvest. Some people may be skeptical about this and I can understand that, so for now, I invite you to just try it. Try speaking positively and thinking positively, growing in your relationship with Christ and the Spirit and see where you are (and how things around you may have changed) after a week, two weeks, three weeks, a month and more. Again, use your journal to document your experiences and things you can see and sense shifting. Often, things will begin shifting in a way that you can only sense, you cannot yet see them tangibly shifting.

If you feel something is holding you back, pray about it and let the Spirit talk to you and guide you on this. Try to answer the following questions: what is holding me back? Why do I feel a bit of a resistance to doing this? How does the Spirit suggest and guide me regarding dealing with these shifts? Am I willing to follow through on what the Spirit is guiding me to do? Make sure you record your answers. Documenting is very important.

_____

_____

_____

5

The Company We Keep

This is very important. The company we keep is so completely important and has a big effect on who we become. How so? Because we are social creatures and we can and will be influenced by the company we keep.

In Scripture, it warns against keeping bad company: *"Keep company with the wise and you will become wise. If you make friends with stupid people, you will be ruined."* (Proverbs 13:20) This means that we have to be very careful about who we spend time with and whom we choose to listen to and take advice from. I don't know about you but when my friends and I talk to each other, we tend to listen and give each other advice. We tend to listen to that advice more frequently when it comes from a person who is in our close inner-circle. I also want to point out that as such, we have to pray hard and meaningfully about who we choose to let into our inner circle.

I recall many years ago when I was first coming to Christ, this advice was provided to me and I sensed early-on that the Lord was guiding me to reconsider some of my friendships. He was guiding me to realize that some people in my life did not have my best interests at heart and were not people with whom I should be associating. I thought therefore about the advice some of these people had given me in the past and here are some examples of the not-so-great choices that I had made previously and where, true to the information about the boat's rudder in the previous chapter, I had to change course:

- Encouraging me to get into new age practices
- Encouraging me to buy new age resources
- Encouraging me to be promiscuous and "just have sex without worrying about it"
- Guiding me to join the pro-choice movement
- Discouraging me from taking time to pray and read my Bible
- Encouraging me to try promiscuous dancing
- Telling me there would be nothing wrong with marrying the man I had met online
- Offering to take a new age course with me

It is only when we take time to really critically think and reflect that we can see peoples' good influence on us or their negative influence on us. It is also really important to value ourselves as daughters of Christ (since this book was written solely for the female) and to find our worth in Him, so that we do not allow ourselves to do things that will devalue us and that will allow us to adopt people's views that we are "less than".

We are Christ's daughters and we need to be secure in that. When we let the wrong people into our social circles, we allow negative to seep in and that negative will try to get a firm grasp and hold on us. So whom do we let in? People who are life-affirming, who lead us and encourage us in the right ways and people who understand and affirm our value in Christ and that the Holy Spirit tells us we should proceed with.

I recall having a friend whom I will name Samaria. We had met through work and she seemed like the nicest person, very personable and easy to talk to, not to mention very kind. She seemed to be floundering in her career a little bit but I sensed that she still had a good head on her shoulders and when she spoke, she regularly spoke life-affirming words. Everything seemed to line up. Then, we got into a discussion about a controversial topic. We had different views on this topic and while I didn't like her view (because I had the opposite one) I didn't want to make an issue about it. I can respect when people hold differing views from my own but still respect my views and why I have them. But she would not let this go. She kept making her points again and again, insisting emphatically that she was right about this and that I had no grounds for my stance. I explained and talked about the moral and faith-based side of the "argument" and that she shouldn't try to change my mind on this topic because I would not be. She could not accept this. She continued to try to change my mind and I really didn't like that, especially when she knew I was strong in faith and said that I didn't want her to continue trying to convince me.

Praying about a friendship is really important because we need to know if this friendship will be good for us now and down the line. Only God will know that and He is not usually hiding this information from us - He wants to tell us so that we can benefit from knowing the information.

Also, just because a person is a Christian (or says they are Christian), it does not mean that you are meant to be friends with them. God will guide you as to whether friendship with them is the best thing but we have to ask explicitly (in our minds or by our words) and we have to make sure that we are listening in an open manner, not letting our own desires cloud what He is saying.

He May Also Be Dealing With This

Your future husband may also be dealing with the wrong people being in his crowd of friends and they may be wrongly influencing him. For example, he could have a friend in his crowd that is encouraging him not to take a much-needed step in helping to ensure that he meets you or moves things along with you. For example, Derrick had been praying to meet his future wife and he felt led to go to his local church for one of their social evenings. His friend, Eric, however, was not a believing man and so he continued to encourage Derrick not to go to the church evening but to, instead, go to a bar downtown to "meet chicks." Derrick did not listen to his "friend" and he chose to go to the church social evening where he met Dalia, whom he met and married in less than a year. Derrick had been sensing strongly that he would meet his future wife at that event and sure enough, that did happen.

Some friendships are brought to us by the Lord and some are not. We have to pray to know which is which.

Kara had been promiscuous for most of her adult life. Her mother had taught her that being promiscuous was the only way to keep a man in her life, so Kara continued bed-hopping for years, going from man to man who would use her for pleasure and then ghost her. After years of doing this, Kara had very little self-esteem and felt that she was never going to be able to keep a man. Kara's sister, Rouanna, had sensed that this was not the right way and chose a different path than the one her mother had guided them both to: Rouanna met, fell in love with and married a wonderful, kind and successful lawyer who would give her three happy and healthy children. When I asked Rouanna what made the difference for her and why she had chosen differently from her sister, she explained simply that because of her faith and some common sense, she felt strongly that the advice from their mother was incorrect and that bed-hopping was not going to be the way to find her "meant-for" and to have a long and happy marriage with him. Kara's mother may have meant well but her advice was incorrect and she was causing one of her daughters to be completely misled and to a life of meaningless sexual pursuits, causing the one thing that she had wanted, to be loved unconditionally, to elude her completely.

Steve knew he was in a bad marriage. His wife treated him like garbage, speaking to him disrespectfully and despite his having said that he wanted children and her agreeing to that, she refused to stop taking her birth control and to get on-route to their first pregnancy. Steve felt trapped and knew there was better for him out there but didn't know where to look or what to do. A friend invited him to church with him and he decided to go. The pastor's sermon that day was about the right person. Steve felt very grateful because he felt this could help him - nothing else had been. After the service, Steve and his friend got to talking about the sermon and his friend took time to answer Steve's questions. His friend wisely pointed out that the right woman would not berate Steve the way his wife had been and continued to and would not make Steve feel bad about his desires to have children. He reminded Steve that he did not grow up in church but that he clearly had a desire for children (and to be respected) that his wife neither supported nor appreciated. Steve's friend gave him some resources he could listen to on this topic. Steve's biggest worry was that God hates divorce therefore no matter how bad things got with his wife, he could never divorce her.

Then, Steve started listening to the sermons his friend had given him and he began a close, personal relationship with Christ. He learned about Christ's love for him, Christ having died for his sins and realized that while the Lord hates divorce, He also hates it when we marry the wrong person because that means we are not living our right life. Steve had other people in his life who would openly mock his desire to be treated correctly by his wife and who would openly mock his reading the Bible. He began to see some trends in how some people were treating him versus how others were. Steve made the choice to only allow those people into his life who were 1) treating him with consistent respect and 2) who were supportive of his decision to follow faith

As Steve started to make better quality decisions for his life, he began to see some real and important changes take place, ones that affirmed his identity in Christ. As his self-esteem and self-confidence grew, Steve began making choices that reflected those changes.

Andrew felt torn between two loves that he had grown up with, Martha and Loewen. He felt strongly for them both and they had both told him they were serious about him so he knew he had to make a choice. He loved Martha's sense of humor and how easy it was to be with her, but also appreciated Loewen's sense of duty and care as she had an ailing dad. He was torn. His friends were all telling him to choose Martha because she was the hotter one. There was no other real rationale for his friends influencing him and encouraging him to get together with Martha. Finally, Andrew went to church to see his pastor. He was looking for proper guidance and direction and sensed that he was not going to find that with his friends. The pastor encouraged Andrew to pray about it and to allow God to choose the right woman. He pointed out that God knew both of these women intimately from birth and that He was in the best position to help Andrew through this decision.

Andrew decided to pray about it. Not once but many times and the more he spent time alone with the Lord, the more he could see that only one of these women was always there for him, only one of them always went above and beyond to help him, to care for him, to talk to him about his problems, to pray with him. Only one of them always told him how great he was despite all the problems he was having and despite the fact that he was a flawed man just like any other person. He could see that one of them loved him the way that would be needed in a solid marriage. He could see that only Martha had visited him when he was in the hospital with a ruptured appendix and had prayed for him when he was about to be wheeled into surgery.

Now, Loewen may have had some wonderful qualities as well, but God knows Loewen's heart and whom He created for her. It was not Andrew.

Readers, it is very important to keep company in our lives who understand and affirm our faith and who support and encourage our relationship with Christ. I am not saying that your only friends or the only company you keep has to be Christians, but they need to be people who will encourage your faith journey in Christ and who will support that you are making choices based on how Christ is guiding you.

In the example above, there were clearly people in Steve's life who were not doing that and who were bringing him down, causing him to have forgotten his identity in Christ. As such, day after day, week after week, year after year, these people were actively chipping away from his best life, causing him to make decisions that were not in his best interest.

Another great example of pursuing your best identity in Christ: Aneta was a happily married woman. She loved and deeply respected her husband of 5 years, Ronald, whom she had met in high school and had remained devoted to him throughout their college years and then later, when they were married. Ronald, on the other hand, did not have the same values as Aneta and he would go out frequently without her, sometimes sharing a motel room with other women. Aneta's friends saw this happening and were trying to explain to her that her husband was not as devoted to her as she was to him but Aneta was having a hard time internalizing that and accepting it. Aneta turned to a cult to get her validation, upon the suggestion of a "friend". She began going to the meetings and following their principles. One of Aneta's closest friends (a woman she had known since high school) did not like what was happening to her friend so she began praying deeply for her. She began praying for Aneta's eyes to be opened to all that was really going on around her. Slowly, Aneta's devout Christian sister, Marianna, came back into her life after they had been estranged for years. Marianna had also sensed that Aneta needed her and reached out. When she saw how far Aneta had gone, she came back into her life in an active way to help her sister see all that was needed to be seen. Marianna began to remind Aneta of her worth and how her husband was not demonstrating any devotion to her. Aneta began to see that and so she asked her husband to go to counseling with her. He begrudgingly agreed and in therapy, his lack of respect for her slowly started to come out. Being the kind and forgiving woman Aneta is, she told her husband that she forgave him for the areas where he faltered but the thing is, Ronald was not looking for forgiveness. He told Aneta that he appreciated her love for him but that he was choosing to go in another direction and no longer wanted to be married to her. Aneta felt the wind be knocked out of her and upon the helpful advice of Marianna, Aneta decided she would attend church more often in an effort to discover her identity in Christ. She wanted to look for the man who would appreciate her and all that she had to offer.

Praying Bold Prayers

When we are not seeing things changing for the better, and we may feel stuck, we sometimes need to pray more bold prayers. Bold prayers mean that we are relying on the solid promises of God and we are making our requests clear that we are in agreement with what God wants for us so we are asking for our bold prayer to be manifested. Praying bold prayers is important and sometimes, we do need to be more assertive in our prayers and in letting God know that we know He is on the throne, He is capable of doing anything and that nothing stands in His way.

Why is this necessary? Because there may be times when darkness gives us a run for our money and makes life really difficult, throwing many obstacles in our way. It is therefore really important to have conviction for praying for the things God has put on our hearts.

Taking this point further, just as God wants us to be with this right person, the darkness does not want us to be with this right person, so they will often bring you another option who seems really great on the surface but when you dig in deeper, you will see the lies and the deception. In my earlier example of the man I met online who was not right for me, I found out later on that he had cheated on me several times - something I did not find out until our relationship was officially done. It seemed great on the surface but it ended up being terrible for me.

Continuing To Pray

(1 Thessalonians 5:16-18) **16** *Rejoice always,* **17** *pray continually,* **18** *give thanks in all circumstances; for this is God's will for you in Christ Jesus.*

Praying once is great. But if you are looking for a real connection with God, to get your prayers continually answered and looking for God's power in your life, praying once will not be sufficient. We need to get into the practice of praying regularly and to using as much detail as possible in our prayers.

A pastor whom I had met once asked me if she thought it was acceptable to pray for such things as wealth and abundance. She had said that she and her spouse had felt the call of duty to begin a school and that they were not to charge much for the school's tuition. There is nothing wrong with that and God has many ways of bringing you the funds and the resources for anything He has called you to do. There are many people I know whom He has guided to a more modest life but there is also nothing wrong with having an abundance mentality and praying for that and making sure that we are taking the right and responsible actions to achieve that.

The Team of You and Him and Him

As this is a book about preparing to say "I do", I feel it's a worthwhile point in time to mention that the man He will bring you will be one whom God has selected to help compliment one another in achieving the lifestyle He has called you to. For example, if He has called you to an abundance lifestyle with significant financial resources, He is going to bring you a man that compliments your ways of doing things. Where you may be good at negotiating but maybe lacking in envisioning something more grand, your husband-to-be may be really good at envisioning and therefore will be able to balance you out and be able to provide that input.

To illustrate, Jane felt deeply that she was called to do ministry in the most remote parts of Africa. She felt a deep sense of empathy for the areas that had no running water and that were not well-equipped with sanitation services. The man whom God brought her, Jerry, was an engineer and was exceptionally good and being able to create and install the sanitary infrastructure that would be needed to get to cleaner sanitation. Jane was excellent at connecting with the locals (which was very much needed) while Jerry was really good at instructing the locals on how to use the newly-installed sanitation systems. In addition, it is not every spouse who would be keen to support their wife in such an endeavor. Many things have to line up for that to be the case and for both people to go on a missions trip like that.

On the other hand, Jake is brilliant in business. He works in real estate and has a great eye for properties. Monica is also really good at real estate but she possesses a quality that Jake was lacking - she is very good at reading through the fine print on contracts and is able to re-word a clause that does not work well for them. Jake always leaves this side of the business to Monica and it has always worked very well for them.

Edmondo is a great and brilliant surgeon but he would not come home for days at a time due to the long hours he has to pull at the hospital. Edmondo knows that this is where he was meant to be and he always feels deeply grateful to God for opening up the way for him to practice surgery as often as he does, because these are not only very difficult positions to come by but you also have to be given the opportunity to do so once you are hired by a hospital. Edmondo's ideal match is Rivka. Rivka is the kind of woman who is very comfortable in her skin and has her own interests. As such, she has no problem with the late and long hours Edmondo always puts in at the hospital, sometimes not even coming home because he has surgeries to do.

When you meet someone who compliments you so well and with whom you have an amazing connection, the chances and the likelihood is that that person was brought to you by God. Yes, you may not always see completely eye-to-eye about everything but generally speaking, the right man for you will be the one who compliments and loves things about you that another may not, and where you compliment him and you love things about him that another may not.

In all of the examples given in this chapter, each of the men and women had previously met people who lacked a real understanding and appreciation for them, their work, their passions and their ways. They had previously met people who did not compliment them well and this can lead to many more difficulties than a marriage needs to have.

6

When You Aren't Sure...Get Confirmation

There may be some ladies reading this who feel they may have heard from the Holy Spirit but they are not sure. They may feel that they are receiving guidance but they are not sure. What do you do in that situation? You journal and you get fellow Christians to check your journaling.

Having Christians who can give you a sense of whether you are hearing from the Holy Spirit is really important and really helps to make sure you are on the right path. Biblically, we were advised to have such safeguards, in the form of helpers and counselors, those willing to help us ensure that we are on the right path.

Now, I want to be clear here about 2 things:

1) You are not asking them what they think of your journaling. No. You are asking them if their Spirit bears witness that the

journaling you have written is from the Holy Spirit or if you are being deceived.

2) Select your checkers very carefully and ask God to help you ensure that you have selected the right people. I say that because if the people looking over your personal journaling are not operating out of the right intentions, well then you are setting yourself up for failure. Having these safety guards is very helpful and really makes a grand difference in helping one to not get deceived. After all, there is little worse than realizing on step 10 that you are and you have been moving in the wrong direction. I don't know about you but I would rather find that out in step 1 or 2 so that I can go back and fix things quickly.

Journal checkers need to be people you really trust and you have prayed over to trust with your journaling. After all, you are sharing with these people an important part of your life and you need to be certain (before you send them your journaling) that they are on the same page in terms of your expectations, timelines, and how they are to respond.

Ask Specifically

I was speaking with a lovely Christian woman who said that she never heard from the Holy Spirit the way that I was able to: in clear, cohesive sentences. Immediately the answer of why she hadn't heard directly came to my mind: "Have you ever asked the Lord to speak to you that way?" I asked her that and she admitted that in her recollection, she didn't believe she ever had asked for that specifically.

You see, for those reading this who may not know this, God is a respecter of your privacy. He will help but you need to ask. You will need to ask Him to do something specific for you, otherwise He will not get involved. So ask specifically and ask more than once. In the Bible, Jesus said that if we ask in His name, He will do it, but it doesn't say He will do it after you ask one or two times, He just He will do it. So, I can tell you from my past experiences that we do need to ask more than once. In fact, when we take the time to ask more than once, we are letting God know that 1) we are relying on Him and depending on Him 2) that this is important enough to us so we are asking more than once or twice 3) we are communicating that this is priority in our lives and to feel free to please talk to us about it and guide us with His truth about this

The Truth....SO Invaluable

This is a great time in the book to highlight and point out how important it is to receive truth. Truth in knowing who God is, truth in understanding how God helps us and operates in our lives, truth in understanding who the right man for you and for the next person is and so many truth pieces.

If you have ever been lied to before, you will further understand how important it is to receive factual information. There are many lies in the world tells us each day, each hour sometimes, but God is not a liar, Jesus is not a liar, the Holy Spirit is not a liar. They are entities that will tell you the truth at all times and that is invaluable, especially when it comes to something like telling you the truth about whom you are meant to marry. This is a topic directly tied to your heart and if you have ever been in a relationship or had your heart broken, you know how important (and the ramifications) of this decision are.

Who you marry is one of the most important decisions you will ever make in your life. It is not a decision to take lightly and it is really important that you realize that people who may be guiding you to "find him using this avenue or that one" may mean very well, but they may not be connected to God and therefore inspired by the Holy Spirit so they may not be guiding you to where you are supposed to meet him.

The Story of Becca

Becca was a lovely and very kind young woman in her thirties. She wore her heart on her sleeve and she found it very important to treat others kindly and with respect (certainly admirable qualities). Becca was looking for the man she was supposed to marry, but while she considered herself a Christian, she did not know anything about finding your husband with the help of the Holy Spirit, so when she set out to find him, she listened to the advice of those around her to "just go online" and she met Arto. Arto treated her well enough and found Becca lovely and interesting, so Becca figured this was the right person. You see, Becca had been berated by her father for being overweight for many years and so she had a poor self-concept; she almost didn't believe that she deserved better than a man who would consistently put her down and make her feel ugly because her father had always made her feel so. So when Arto didn't make her feel completely ugly and treated her decently, she immediately thought "let me not let this man go". Becca married

Arto and it was a disaster of a marriage. They were never on the same page, he enjoyed doing things that Becca hated and wanted no part in, she hadn't learned to handle finances before so they quickly lost their marital home to the bank and more. Arto believed in a strong marriage so they went to counseling together. In their counseling sessions, Becca and Arto began to reveal more and more of who they were to each other and to the counselor and it became clear and plain to see how unsuited they were for each other and how there was a real lack of love between the two.

When the counselor finally asked Becca (in a private session) why she had married Arto, she replied simply "I didn't think I could ever do any better." The counselor pointed out that Becca needed to do some work on herself before making any other big decisions about her future. She could see that Becca's self-concept and view of self were terrible and that she was not going to find her happiness with another until she found it for herself.

There are many issues within the case of Becca and Arto but the one that is most important for the purpose of this section's teaching is that if we don't develop that close relationship with the Holy Spirit and find guidance from Him, then we are setting ourselves up for disappointment. People, as well intentioned as they may be, simply don't know God's plan for our lives unless they ask Him and unless they are in the practice of hearing from the Holy Spirit clearly and accurately, so they simply won't be able to guide us properly.

An Example of Journaling

There may be women reading this who have never journaled before and so they aren't sure what it looks like or how it's supposed to be done. I'd like to provide just a bit of journaling here to give a sense of what it could look like. Remember, journaling can look different from one person to the other mainly because God has a special relationship with each of us and speaks to each person differently but journaling with God will always be kind, respectful, full of love, meaningful and full of hope. Journaling with the Holy Spirit will never berate you, put you down, call you names, be unloving or lack hope. God always loves us so much and will let us know that time and time again.

So, here is an example of what journaling looks like, beginning with a general question (all the writing in italics are from the Holy Spirit).

Me: Holy Spirit, what do You want to say to the women reading this?

H.S.: Fantastic question - I want to tell them how invaluable they are, how beautiful, intelligent and wonderful they are and how much I love each and every one of them. I want to be clear on how important each one is to me. I dwell inside of them following baptism and I am there, dwelling inside of them and there to guide them, support them and show them the way.

Me: How is any woman, lady, female supposed to know about you and tap into all that is offered in you?

H.S.: Simple. They only need to ask Me to talk to them, to speak to them, to guide them, to help them and to consult with Me for anything and everything that they need. They only need to ask and I will be there, helping them and guiding them to the truth. Many women out there do not know about Me or are not familiar enough with Me because there is not enough teaching out there about Me and so they don't know enough about how to tap into Me. Take yourself as an example: until you were fully taught how to tap into Me, you didn't know enough about Me and you didn't know how to tap into all the resources that were available in Me.

Me: So unless one takes courses or something of the like, how are they supposed to tap into You?

H.S.: Using resources such as this book and other resources that teach them about Me. I am an invaluable asset because as you said, there are many lies out there in the world, so tapping into Me as a truth-teller is so important. If women don't tap into Me and ask God for help through Me, they are, in fact, setting themselves up for disappointment. I long to be used by women to show them and to help them, to lead them and to guide them. All of these attributes of Mine are extremely important and if a woman (because this book is geared specifically to women) does not use Me, she will be misguided. That is fact.

Me: So women need to be better educated on how to tap into You and to ask You to speak to them, the same way I am.

H.S.: They must. Life was always designed to be worked on in tandem with Me and so when you don't tap into Me, every woman is leaving out an important part of the equation, thus allowing themselves to be deceived.

Me: What is something else You would like women reading this to know?

H.S.: Many things: I love each of them infinitely, I want each woman to know all the love and the help that is available in Me, I want each to know that they are invited to tap into Me and to see all that is available in Me. I want each woman to know how important they are to Me and why (as in the gifts God has put inside of each woman). There is awesomeness and beauty put into and invested into each woman - Father God and Jesus have put that beauty in there and so it is really important for women to realize that no matter their size, their color, their shape or anything else, that each woman has that beauty in her and needs to realize how amazing she is. And the saying "there is a pot for each lid is true" - there is that special man out there for each woman. Now, every woman is not necessarily meant to be married but God has designed everything so that each woman can have her happy, but she has to want it and accept it because God has given each person free will. God knows each person very well and has provided for each person so if one woman is thinking that that special man is not out there for them, I am here to tell her otherwise. As long as she accepts what God has provided (and what He has provided for her is best) then she will have her God-provided man.

Me: Is there anything else You want to tell women in this section? Any other messages You want me to pass on to my readers?

H.S.: Yes, certainly. I love love love each woman reading this and I love love love each woman who has not had an opportunity to read this. God is a God of love and He has such a special love for each female He has created and put on this earth. That is no small thing because He is an infinite God so you can imagine just how much love He has for each woman He has created. You can imagine just how much love He has and I have and Jesus has for each lady, big or tall, small or large, black or white, and all variations of shapes, sizes and colors. Also, women, love yourselves, cherish yourselves, be good to yourselves because God longs to be good to each of you. He desires to give you the desires of your heart because He has given you the desires that dwell in your heart but many women have to understand the difference between what the enemy has put on their hearts versus what God has put on their hearts, because they will be different.

Me: Thank You, Holy Spirit. Anything else?

H.S.: Yes. Have faith, ladies. It is the cornerstone of life. It is vitally important to tap into the ways of God because no other way is better. Get close to God, invite Me into your life, take in and benefit from all that is available in Me and remember that self love is your reflection of how God loves and sees you. One more thing: for those whom God has put a desire for children on or in your hearts, love them and know that each one is a gift from Me, no matter what. I love each of you with an everlasting love. Thanks.

7

Being Committed Before You Are Committed

When the Holy Spirit has revealed to you who the right man for you is, and lets you know that he needs some work right now or you do, a word of caution to stay committed to praying for him and doing the work assigned to you instead of going out and looking to meet others. We cannot be committed to a lifelong relationship with this man when we are going out and looking (or entering sexual relations) with others.

Jane shared with me one time that she knew God was leading her to Jeremy but that Jeremy needed to work on himself a little bit before entering into such a committed relationship as marriage. In waiting, Jane shared that she didn't see the harm in going out and meeting other men, taking a "sample" of what else is out there before "settling in" with Jeremy. She rationed that "I am just taking a look around in a non-serious way to see what else is out there and if another catches her fancy, but not in a serious way." The Holy

Spirit was speaking to her quite powerfully that that wasn't the way she was supposed to be doing things.

Jane was trying to look around when she was supposed to be preparing for life with Jeremy. Preparing for life with Jeremy, as this book points out, is meant to be a time where you are working on yourself with the Holy Spirit, praying for your husband-to-be and making sure that you develop the skills that will be necessary for marriage. It is not an opportune time to go out and look for others, even if it is for casual encounters. When you are fortunate enough to have the Holy Spirit guide you to a particular man, we need to be cognizant enough of how special that is and we need to make sure that we are doing the work required.

Marriage is WORK

Marriage was always, is and always will be work. It takes all of the following:

- Commitment
- Praying
- Caring
- Being mindful
- Patience
- Understanding
- Consideration
- Much love
- Respect for the other
- Respect for self
- Compassion

- Being "there"

Knowing this, we have to recognize that marriage takes work. It takes commitment and it takes perseverance and on those days when it is challenging, we have to exercise extra amount of care and patience and compassion. There will be days when even the most in-love couple has to work really hard at making their marriage work and there will be days when you both may need a break from one another. We cannot be that committed if we are going out to meet other men, even if it is just for fun or a temporary distraction.

I also want to point out that some couples engage in sharing their partner with others. Respectfully, this is not likely to lead to a happily committed marriage.

So, commitment means committed. It means that you are remaining true to that person and you are willing to sacrifice and do the work that you are being called to do to continue putting time and effort and resources into this man in particular. Can it sometimes be hard? Certainly. But we need to get out of the mentality that going outside of our committed relationship and later, our committed marriage is ok. We need to get it out of our minds that being less than fully committed is ok. Even before we are married, we have to support our men completely and they need to support us. This means and requires doing the work on ourselves and supporting the other person through all stages of their development, remaining committed to them the entire time.

A woman I was speaking to whom I will name Martha was sharing that the man whom she believed the Holy Spirit was guiding her to, Robert, had some issues he needed to work out. Robert had been honest with Martha about the struggles he had with alcohol and that he needed some time to heal and get better before entering into a committed marriage relationship with her. Martha had it in her mind that it was ok to continue looking around while he was in treatment, in case she finds "someone better with more to offer her." I asked Martha if she felt that this was really the way the Holy Spirit was guiding her. She had said that she hadn't tapped into the Spirit and while I encouraged her to do so, she made the decision to go her own way with that and to see other men. Eventually, Robert felt healthy enough to include Martha in his healing process and knew that Martha needed to be party to his healing, so that she could understand what he was dealing with and how he was trying to get healthy. Unfortunately, because Martha was not waiting patiently and in a committed way, she missed this communication from Robert, which hurt Robert tremendously. He felt betrayed because he was going through so much and willing to share his life and his struggles with Martha, who was neither mentally available nor was she emotionally or physically there for him.

Because she had decided not to be committed to Robert during his time of self-improvement, she had missed a critical opportunity to be wife-like and to support him through such a critical time. Robert understood that while he didn't expect her to be there and "at the ready" for when he was ready for her, he did expect that a woman who was serious about him for marriage would have been there for him in a more active way during a time of major trial.

If You Are Serious, Be There

I wish for this to sound supportive: one of the ways that we show a man how serious and how committed we will be to them during marriage is to show them how serious and how committed we will be to them before marriage. If the Holy Spirit has spoken to you and you know the importance of this man in your life, does it not make sense to be as committed to him prior to marriage as it would be to be committed to him during marriage? Of course, I do want to be mindful that you undoubtedly have your own things going on - worries, work, family, friends, etc. - this idea of being there for him is not meant to sound preachy or disrespectful to the long list of things you have to do. There will always be many things in life that keep us busy but your future husband may very well need you to be there for him in a grander way or more significant way than he may currently be expressing it. This will therefore require that we introspect a bit and see how we can best be there for him while also maintaining our own lives. The Holy Spirit is there to help, guide and assist you through all of this.

A lady I was speaking to whom I will call Jaza was going through something like this. She had married Roland and they had been together for over 10 years, having had many children together. Jaza was a deeply Christian woman and understood about remaining committed to her husband during such a tough time. She had shared with me that their marriage had hit a major skid when Roland was struggling significantly with some personal issues and felt that his life was going off the rails. Due to his issues, he began to treat Jaza terribly, being very unfair to her. Jaza knew and recognized what was going on and she had shared that while she felt his behavior was unfair, she did understand why he was acting and reacting the way he was and that she needed to be patient and support him through those trials. She shared just how difficult this had all been for them both and how much she wanted life to get back to the happy normal that they previously experienced.

She had made the choice to stand by Roland through these times and she had said how she was actively praying for a solution to his problems, which would then ultimately help get their lives together back on track.

It Takes Spiritual Maturity

I believe that it takes Spiritual maturity to recognize and to understand when your spouse or spouse-to-be is going through difficulties. If we do not understand this point, we are much more likely to think that the person is just being mean or rude or inconsiderate. If we do not understand this point, we are much more likely to think that the person is just being unreasonable or disrespectful and we are likely to just leave.

When we understand the Spiritual dimension, we can better understand what is really at play and how we should be strategically handling it and dealing with it, as opposed to just running for the hills.

There are many self-help books out there teaching women about relationships. But none of the self-help books teach about relying on the Holy Spirit, and that is where a huge piece of the puzzle is basically taken out. Taking the Holy Spirit out of the equation is like saying "I broke my leg and I want to get better but I am never going to go to the doctor who will tell me exactly how I am supposed to get better." Here are some of the names of the Holy Spirit and I give these to you here so that you can understand the important roles He plays in our lives:

- Counselor
- Helper
- Truth teller
- Good Spirit
- Eternal Spirit
- The Lord
- Spirit of the Sovereign Lord
- Spirit of God
- Spirit of your Father
- Spirit of life
- Spirit of grace
- Spirit of prophecy
- Spirit of justice
- Spirit of revelation
- Spirit of glory

So, what happens when we take this very helpful Spirit out of the equation? We are literally working against ourselves. We are literally making life more difficult when we take away our Helper. One has to wonder, therefore, why we would take this Helper out of the equation?

Many women I have spoken to have said that they would listen to their friends over listening to the Holy Spirit because their friends are physically there and can be seen, while the Holy Spirit is not. Reader, with due respect to your friends whom I don't know, they are not the ones God has told you is your helper. They are not the ones God has put inside of you to help you realize the truth and what to do about it. Yes, we are supposed to have fellowship, but the Bible clearly says that the Holy Spirit is the One there to help with everything.

Different Situations Will Mean Commitment Looks Different

Many women find themselves in different situations where they are not yet with their right man. This will necessarily mean that commitment is going to look different from different women. For example, a woman who does not yet know who her mate is supposed to be cannot pray for him using his name, while the woman who does know who he is can pray using his name. A woman who knows the man from before (maybe you were in a romantic or friendship relationship with him before) may be able to pray with more specifics because you know a lot about him already.

Let's say you are a woman whose man is working on himself and you may be fortunate enough that he has chosen to make you a partner in his progress and recovery, so your commitment to him may look like going with him to therapy sessions or him talking to you about his needs and struggles. That will look different than a woman who does not know the name of the man yet.

Let's say you are a woman who is divorced and you are looking for the right one this time. You may have more experience with what a marriage is supposed to look like than a woman who has never been married before and has never lived that life.

Your different situation will mean your level of understanding and possibly commitment may look really different.

Ask the Spirit..."How am I doing?" "Am I on the right track?"

One of my favorite things to do is to check-in with the Holy Spirit and ask such questions as "how am I doing?" "Am I on the right track?" "Am I doing the right things?" When we ask these questions, we are demonstrating our reliance on the Holy Spirit, letting Him know how much we need Him, that we are trusting in His ways and processes, and that we care.

It is no different than when we check-in at work or with friends or family. Ask. "How are we doing?" and are we on the right track? Are we doing the things that need to be done for our goal of……………?Some women, I have come to find, are very afraid to ask these questions. Some have shared with me that they are very afraid to ask because they are not sure what the answer is going to be and therefore, that they may have to face having done something wrong. But isn't it better to know now than to find out in a month or in six months when you are further down the wrong road? Checking-in with the Spirit is really important and I suggest doing it as often as possible, no matter what faith or relationship stage you are in.

We have access to the mind of God and the wisdom of God. Doesn't it make sense that it would be wise to tap into that as often as possible?

A last word about being committed: just because we are committed to him, it doesn't necessarily mean that he will be just as committed to us. This is a reality that one cannot ignore. In other words, you may have faith to stand by him and stay committed to him while he may not and you may find this out in a hard way. The take-away point is you did what you were supposed to do and God sees that. He adds that to your credit, so even if he doesn't maintain the commitment and takes some other action, know that you have done the right thing and that God sees that and He will bless you according to His riches and according to your works.

Nothing we ever do for Him and for His will goes unnoticed or unappreciated.

8

So Blessed

I think it's really important to take a moment out at this point and reflect on:

1. The meaning of marriage to you
2. How blessed we are to have access to this truth-telling Spirit

I'd like to take a moment and ask you to reflect for yourself on the blessing of marriage and on receiving guidance directly from the Lord. Do you ever ask Him about this? Do you ever pray about this, prior to reading this book? If you are married, do you ask Him about how to best handle your marriage or the issues that come up? If you are in waiting, do you ask what you need to be doing while you are waiting? Use the space provided here to respond:

Asking the Spirit for Patience, Help, Courage, Etc.

No matter what point in the process you are at, I believe we all need some help in staying the course. Things happen in life and we can feel overwhelmed, tired, unsure, exhausted, etc., and we are meant to rely on the strength of Jesus to help us through these times. This is another reason we say that marriage was never intended to be a union between just man and wife but a union that has God at its center and one where both man and wife are relying on His strength, His help, His assistance, His reassurance, His guidance and more.

So I ask you: do you ask Jesus for strength through whatever you are going through? Do you ask Him to support you and to carry you when you cannot go on or you feel exhausted? Please remember to be honest when you are answering these questions in honest reflection because you and your mate will benefit from your honesty and then, from the honest work you will be guided to do to work on any issues.

_____
_____
_____
_____
_____
_____
_____
_____
_____
_____
_____
_____
_____
_____
_____
_____
_____

Support Systems

We all need solid friends and family support systems. Support systems help us process facts, help us deal with issues, help us pray and help support us anytime we need help. I will talk more about support systems in this section but one thing I would like to make clear is the distinction between God and support systems. Support systems are the friends and family you can go to to talk about something, lament, vent a frustration, share a happiness and more, but it does not take God's place. God is the first One we need to go to with problems, issues, excitement, etc. God is the One who will be available 24 hours per day, 7 days per week…I don't know of any person who can or would be able to give any person that much time and attention.

 Having said that, let's think and plan whom we are being guided to include in our support system. These are the people you believe (and the Holy Spirit confirms) that would be helpful and resourceful to go to when we need support, a helping hand, a helpful ear, a shoulder, and more.

_____
_____
_____
_____
_____
_____
_____
_____

Remember that I noted earlier how important it is to consult with the Holy Spirit and whom your checkers will be. Your checkers need to be, do and have all of the following:

- Maturity in Christ
- Agree to keep your journaling in complete confidence
- Agree to be honest with you even if it is unpleasant
- Are able to discern fairly quickly
- Are able to get back to you fairly quickly
- Are gentle and kind in their approach
- Will never charge you a penny for this service
- Do their own journaling as well

A lady that I had asked to check my journaling with one time asked me for payment per page that I was sending her. I found that to be extremely inappropriate and chose not to send her any of my journaling.

I now do journal checking for others and never have I once asked (or would ask) for payment to do this. Understand that as a checker, you are being put in an important position of responsibility and it is inappropriate to seek payment or any kind of compensation for this important work.

Ask the Spirit Before You Make Plans

I recall one time I had made plans with a lady I know and had spent some time with in friendship. She had approached me about having coffee together which (I didn't think twice) I opted to do so. We settled on a date and a time when the Lord spoke to me very clearly, asking if I had asked Him if this was the right person to talk to and if that date and time were the right times to see her. I realized that I hadn't asked…I had just moved on my own thought to go. Quickly, the Holy Spirit guided me that her intentions were not as good as she made them seem and that this was not someone who had my best interests at heart. I was floored. I didn't see her that way and had never thought she had any ulterior motive or impure motive to see me. The Lord made it abundantly clear to me that she was not a good friend with good motives and that I needed to cancel the social outing. I did so because I had had enough experience to know that when He guides you to not go ahead with something, He has a very good reason.

So, I canceled the appointment and realized that I had likely just been helped out of what would likely have been a really bad situation.

Reflection: do you ask Him before you do something? If He were to speak and guide you, would you listen and obey or do as you please?

___

Laura

Laura is a lovely 40-something woman who is looking to get married. Her friends, family and colleagues have all offered to set her up with this man and with that one, trying to help her find the one that fits the criteria Laura had set. Laura is a Christian and she believes that God has the right man for her but she also knows what she wants in a man and has never really asked or tapped into the Holy Spirit for guidance and direction. Finally, Laura agrees to date Ernie, a 40-something lawyer and litigator who has one child from a previous marriage (he is now divorced) and who seems to fit all the criteria Laura had said she was looking for. Her coworker Emily had set them up and they were to go for dinner to a very upscale restaurant. Ernie did everything a gentleman should do on a date: he held the car and restaurant doors open for her, he was kind and respectful throughout their date, he complimented her genuinely when he found her and her outfit to be just beautiful, and he asked about her while respecting her privacy and tried not to be intrusive for a first date. Laura really enjoyed spending time with Ernie and hearing about his life, his law practice, even his previous marriage and enjoyed spending time with a gentleman. As the months wore on and Laura went on many more dates with Ernie, she began to develop real feelings for him and he clearly for her as well. He was talking about serious commitments before she knew it and had asked her to move in with him and his child.

What Laura wasn't factoring in with consulting with the Holy Spirit from the beginning. She never asked for insight about this man, she never asked for input on whether this man was the right person for her, according to God's will. Laura chose to get married to Ernie and to become official stepmom to his child, whom she felt a connection with. Unfortunately, because Laura hadn't consulted with the Holy Spirit, she was living a fantasy of lies. Ernie was not in fact divorced, and he was several thousands of dollars in debt. He knew well enough though, that when you get married, your spouse takes on part of that debt, so that's what Ernie did. He left the country and his child and his debts to Laura. He had promised he would return in one year after taking care of some business "back home" but that one year turned into two, which turned into three, and I think you get where I am going with this....

Not consulting with the Holy Spirit cost Laura dearly.

Emmett

This is a book for women but there are examples of unfortunate things that happen to men as well (of course) so we can draw from the experiences of men as well. Emmett was a very kind and sweet IT developer who had a solid relationship with Christ. He was looking to get married and his friend set him up with Christina, who was also in the tech field. Emmett and Christina got along great, going for dates and spending quality time together. Christina had suggested that she and Emmett attend church together in an effort to strengthen both their bond and their bond with Christ. Emmett was really pleased that Christina seemed to be as faith-driven as he, so he said he would gladly go.

At church, the pastor had talked about how we need to follow Christ and how that meant walking away from things when they do not seem right. Emmett felt the pastor speaking directly to his heart but did not understand why. He sensed that this involved his current relationship with Christina but didn't understand how. As time wore on and their relationship continued, Emmett's uneasiness grew. He sensed something was off but didn't know what and so he decided to ask God to make it very clear to him. Emmett prayed and shared with God that he really wanted to get married and wondered if Christina was the right person. He asked God to make this abundantly clear to him, in any way He could. Christina called and asked if they could have dinner. She said she had something important to talk to him about. Emmett felt this was an answer to his prayers so he agreed to dinner, waiting in anticipation to see what Christina would say.

At dinner, Emmett spoke to Christina about the future he felt he saw for himself and how intricate a part of his life he felt God was going to be. Christina began crying. When he asked her what was wrong, she broke down even further in tears and admitted to Emmett that she had not been faithful to him, but that she had been cheating on him with a coworker. Emmett sat there stunned. He had no idea she had been cheating on him but he realized now that this is why he felt so uneasy about everything.

Emmett, being such a kind man, did not want to cause a scene or hurt Christina. He collected himself, thanked her for her honesty and wished her the best of luck with her future, whatever that looked like. He left the dinner and went home to process everything, but felt so thankful to God for having revealed the truth to him, before things went any further.

Chloe

Chloe was a very beautiful, very striking woman. Her eyes were big and green and she had a smile that was just incredible. She had been a model in her earlier days and decided to put that career on the back-burner to focus on her dream of being a marine biologist. She had applied for and got hired as a marine biologist for a large multinational corporation and she was very excited about her first job, that was going to take her to Alaska. She had prayed over this job opportunity and she felt very strongly that the Lord was giving her the proverbial "thumbs up" to take the role. So, she accepted the job, packed her bags and was on her way to Alaska, armed with her previous knowledge and experience.

The job was all that she had hoped it would be and she felt really happy. She was able to take care of the animals, was able to use all her training and felt well-equipped for this, her very first job as a marine biologist. Then things hit a snag. Her boss did not like her. He was rude, mean, condescending and clearly did not think much of her or value her ideas or opinion in any way. She was always looking for ways to impress him with her knowledge or looking for ways to make him to make him like her but nothing was working. She spoke to one of her friends on the phone and asked her for advice, to which her friend said "Did you ask the Holy Spirit to reveal to you why your boss doesn't seem to like you and what you can do about it?" Chloe realized that she had never asked that so she said "Ok, I'll do that!" As she prayed about it, the Holy Spirit revealed to her that it was in fact not what she thought at all. In fact, the Spirit revealed to her that her boss, Massimo, actually liked her romantically, and because he knew he could not act on it because he was her boss, he was treating her as though he didn't like her. She realized it was a cover-up. Chloe, being the very direct woman that she is, decided to confront him, gently. He cracked immediately. He told her about how he had liked her from the beginning because she was astonishingly smart and beautiful but that he knew he couldn't do anything about it because he was her boss.

Chloe was extremely flattered and began to have some feelings for him in return. Again, she spoke to him about this and they decided that following the project (when he would no longer be her boss) they would be able to explore things on a personal level and see what would come of it. She was very excited for the project to end so that they could explore these thoughts and feelings. A few months later, the project did end successfully and she and Massimo were both offered extensions. While they were both excited to take the extension, they both knew they wanted the opportunity to explore their personal relationship so they both decided to postpone that opportunity and to begin dating. They were very in-sync with each other and Chloe sensed the Holy Spirit giving her the thumbs-up to continue. She continued to consult with the Holy Spirit during the entire process and their entire dating time, looking for confirmation on when each step and phase of their personal relationship should take place. She was enjoying herself tremendously, as was Massimo.

You see, friends, by listening to the Holy Spirit within, Chloe (and Massimo) benefited in many ways. She was led and was successful in exploring and establishing a new career, in dealing with her unfair boss and in beginning and continuing a personal, romantic relationship with him. She consulted with the Spirit each step of the way and this served her very well.

Marianna

Marianna knew she had a book in her. Estonian writing and grammar had been passions of hers for a very long time and she was excited about the process and then of the finished result, which she had hoped would help many Estonians and those who spoke

Estonian benefit from her experiences and writing. The problem was that life was getting in the way. She had many responsibilities, from work to caregiving and then being a foster parent and much more. She felt she would never have the time to write this book and she felt that she would never have the opportunity to get this book out to the public. She figured she would write when she had the opportunity, after retirement. Her family Eisa had a chat with her. She asked Marianna how things were going in life and with the book that she knew Marianna wanted to write and publish. Marianna explained that she had way too many responsibilities and that it wasn't the right time to do that. Eisa asked her if she had prayed about it. She asked her if she had asked God if now was the right time to write it. Marianna admitted that she had not asked and so she had no idea if now was the right time or not, so she got to praying about it. Sure enough, the Spirit came powerfully over Marianna and spoke to her very clearly that this was the perfect time to write her book and that she must get started right away. Marianna prayed, explaining to the Spirit that she had no time to do this and the Spirit guided her to just get started and that He would open the way for her. So, she did. She took out her laptop and began writing the first few lines, despite the phone ringing, despite all her responsibilities - she found a few minutes here and there to write, but no significant amounts of time. Slowly but assuredly, the Spirit began moving circumstances out of her way: Eisa offered to take the kids to the park 3 days per week for an hour each time so that Marianna could write, Marianna's mother stepped up and took on more of a caregiving role that Marianna would otherwise have had to do, and Marianna asked if she could work from home for part of the time - a request that was immediately granted. All of a sudden, a bunch of time had just opened up for her.

Readers, do not work in your own efforts alone and in your own wisdom alone. You do not need to. Work as partners with God through all that you are doing because when you work with Him and partner with Him, you are 1) accessing His infinite wisdom for all situations and 2) you are activating His power within a situation

I have said this before and will say it again: we were never meant to do life completely on our own. We were always meant to do it in tandem with the One who created us and who knows us best.

How will you tap into the Holy Spirit today?
_____
_____
_____
_____
_____
_____
_____
_____
_____
_____
_____
_____
_____
_____
_____
_____
_____

9

How the Lord Speaks

God speaks to us in a variety of ways. Here are each of them:

- Through Scripture - (2 Timothy 3:16-17) *"All Scripture is God-breathed and is useful for teaching, rebuking, correcting and training in righteousness, so that the servant of God may be thoroughly equipped for every good work"*
- Through gifted teachers whose source is the Bible (Romans 12:6-8) *"We have different gifts, according to the grace given to each of us. If your gift is prophesying, then prophesy in accordance with your faith; if it is serving, then serve; if it is teaching, then teach; if it is to encourage, then give encouragement; if it is giving, then give generously; if it is to lead, do it diligently; if it is to show mercy, do it cheerfully"*
- God speaks to us through difficulties (Psalm 119:67-68) *"Before I was afflicted I went astray, but now I obey your word. You are good, and what you do is good; teach me your decrees"*

- God speaks to us through the Holy Spirit (John 14:26) *"But the Advocate, the Holy Spirit, whom the Father will send in my name, will teach you all things and will remind you of everything I have said to you"*
- God speaks through His creation (Psalm 19:1-2) *"The heavens declare the glory of God; the skies proclaim the work of his hands. Day after day they pour forth speech; night after night they reveal knowledge"*
- God speaks to us through whatever and whenever He chooses, but it will always agree with His Word (Job 33:14) *"For God does speak — now one way, now another — though no one perceives it"*

God loves to speak to us in different ways, making sure that He gets His points across. But we need to tune in. If we don't tune in, how are we ever going to hear Him properly? The enemy does not want us to hear God properly because that will limit him and his powers in our lives. If we turn away from God or we stop making listening to Him a priority, we are playing directly into the schemes of the enemy.

There will be times when we do not understand what God is doing - I have certainly been there many times myself. In those cases, we have to rely on the personality and goodness of God - His reputation. He does not lie, He does not steal, He is good all the time and He will only ever want the best for us. So in those moments where it may not make sense, we have to rest on that - His character of being so good.

In Proverbs 3:5-6, we are presented with the passage *"Trust in the Lord with all thine heart; and lean not unto thine own understanding. In all thy ways acknowledge Him, and He shall direct thy paths."* I can't express enough how important this Scripture is. We are not able to see everything or know everything. Only He is so when He guides us in ways that we would never have thought of or He shows us ways that don't seem to make any sense to us, it is because He is guiding us via His ways because He sees the plans and potential pitfalls all around us.

Praying for Loved Ones

I remember praying some time ago for any plans for harm or destruction against my family to be wiped away. I remember praying very clearly for the Lord to look after all members of my family and to thwart the plans of the enemy.

A few weeks later, my dad was going to a routine dermatologist appointment. My mom was conveying to me later on that the dermatologist noticed something on my dad's back that she didn't like the look of. She proceeded to get rid of it and to send it to the lab for testing. A few days later, she called with the results. Sure enough, it was cancer. The dermatologist got rid of the entire thing and said that it was caught very early, otherwise it would have progressed to a stage 1 level. I am certain that this was part of the enemy's plan against my dad and that my prayer for God's protection had foiled the plans of the enemy.

Readers, as we sit, write, eat, talk, go to work, be social, be with our family, enjoy our friends, the enemy is plotting against us. We have to be mindful and vigilant of this because if we are not, the plans will come to fruition. It's like if you don't close the door to your home, you may not necessarily have a big sign on your lawn saying "come in, rob us" but by not closing the door to your home, you are letting the possibility of unfortunate things come to you. We have to always be vigilant about this because we are literally talking about life and death.

Unique

God has a unique and special relationship with each of us. We are all different in some ways and He always likes to have that personal relationship with each of His children. The way He speaks to me may not be the way He will (or does) speak to you.

I recall a good friend sending me her journaling for confirmation. As I was reading through it, I could see how differently He was speaking with her than He does with me. I could see how He used fancier words with her, His pauses and level of detail with her were much different than communication with me and so on. I felt happy about that because I preferred the more casual ways He spoke to me - the way He speaks to me is exactly the way I would want Him to - clear, uncomplicated and to the point.

How does He speak to you? Do you feel you ever hear from Him? Does He speak to you in very informal ways? Write down your responses here:

_____
_____
_____
_____
_____
_____
_____
_____
_____
_____
_____
_____
_____
_____
_____
_____

Scripture That Jumps Out At You

When you are reading Scripture, you may get a verse or verses that jump out at you. That is God speaking to you as well, letting you know that this is particularly relevant and relates to your life. It is one of the main ways God speaks to us and lets us know a message about that thing. A wise thing to do would be to jot that down somewhere and to write down the question "What are You wanting to tell me about this?" or "God, is there something particularly important that You are trying to tell me about with this Scripture?"

Asking the Lord to be super clear: no matter what stage in your walk with God you are in, it is important to ask Him to be super clear about His communication with you. Ask Him clearly to talk to you clearly about something and to bring something to your attention, as well as to ask for confirmation from Christian sources that the communication is from Him. Having advisors around you is very important and this should never be something a person charges you for.

Sometimes, just spending time alone with Him in nature is a great way for Him to speak to you. To someone else, it could just be a babbling brook but to you, it could mean so much more. To someone else, the birds chirping in the sky could be lovely but ordinary but to you, it could mean so much more. He speaks to us through nature all the time. Stay open to that communication or to those communications.

Warning, Warning, Warning

I will never forget how one ordinary summer day, I felt the warning of God so very clearly and it was like it was on repeat. I felt the warning strongly that someone was about to come into my life and that I was to be very cautious of that person, that they would mean no good for my life. I remember how many times the warning repeated itself and how clear and strong it was.

Then the problem happened: I forgot about the warning.

I went about my daily life and sure enough, a new man came into my life. He seemed great on the surface: charming, sweet, very attractive and smart. He seemed to be the whole package. I had completely forgotten about the warning I had received and forgot about how strongly the Lord had warned me about him. A flirtation began. Then we got closer. And then we started texting all the time. He seemed wonderful. As time went on, my desire for him grew and it was only months later, when he completely turned on me and seemingly-became a different person that I realized just how wrong I had been about him. It was not until after I felt completely emotionally destroyed that I realized that God had warned me many times about him and that I did not pay attention. Well, I certainly paid for that one. Hindsight is 20-20 and I realized how not heeding the warnings of God would lead to total destruction.

Right Thing, Wrong Timing

There is such a thing as right things, wrong timing. If something is right but it is within the wrong timing, then it really should be avoided. Something that has the wrong timing will end up devastating us because the wrong timing implies all of the following:

- it is not ripe yet for picking
- the thing has not yet matured

- when something is in development, it implies that it will be making mistakes along the way and you may end up getting in the line of fire of that
- lack of respect unto you - when something is in the process of maturing, it means that it is in process and therefore, is still developing. This necessarily implies that it will neither have the time nor will it have the attention to give you the full attention and respect you deserve. As such, again, you may end up getting in the line of fire for that

As someone is maturing (this could also mean if a person is developing), give them the time and the space to do so. Let them have that space to develop, to realize things and to come into the fullness of who they are. Give them the room to grow because growing necessarily means that they will make some mistakes.

Goosebumps

Every time Flora got near Shawn, she would get goosebumps. She was completely perplexed by this and didn't understand why that was happening. Every time he would call, stop by or they would "hang out" and go for coffee, she would get goosebumps. She couldn't figure out why this was happening so she decided to pray about it. The Lord spoke to her very clearly and let her know that this was His way of letting her know that she had met her match - the man that was right for her. She was impressed that the Lord had used this unique method to get that message to her and to let her know something so important.

Your Conscience

Your conscience is another way God speaks to you. If your conscience is bothering you, that means something you have done or said is not "sitting well with you". It means that something is out of alignment.

Roula was having a conscience attack. She was feeling very uneasy and felt bad about her most recent conversation with her mom. She didn't know why this time she felt so bad about it - they had had many disagreements (even arguments) in the past but this time, she felt significantly worse about it. Roula had her ways of doing things but her mother did not agree with her and was trying to make Roula understand why. The conversation had taken an ugly turn when Roula began accusing her mother of such things as being controlling, unfair and not respecting her space or her choices. Roula had begun screaming at her mother out of frustration but was feeling really bad about it this time. Roula began praying for wisdom about why she was feeling so bad and she got a vision of a very bad and serious car accident. She prayed further to inquire about what this accident was about and who was involved in it. Immediately, the Lord spoke to Roula and encouraged her to pray for her mother who had been in a very bad accident. The Spirit had let her know that her mom had gone out in anger and in frustration and had been driving very recklessly. Immediately, Roula got on her knees and began praying for her mom and her mom's well-being. Thirty minutes later, Roula got a call from the paramedics saying that her mother had been in a very serious accident and that she needed to get to the intensive care very quickly. She may not make it through the hour.

As Roula rushed to the hospital, she prayed to the Lord to save her mom. She prayed for the Lord to mend her mother in any ways that were needed and that she would have another opportunity to talk to her mom again and to apologize to her for the way she had spoken to her.

Readers, when the Holy Spirit speaks to us, He may do so through your conscience, letting you know something is wrong. Don't ignore that. Don't ignore the prompts that you are getting because that is one important way God speaks to us and lets us know something is not right.

In the case of Roula, her prayers were answered and her mother pulled through the car accident. Roula did get an opportunity to apologize to her mom and to let her know that she wanted to start a more open, loving and healthy relationship with her. Her mom was delighted.

10

Vision Boards

Vision boards with Jesus at the center are terrific.

Vision boards are such a great tool to help make concrete the things that the Holy Spirit is showing you and to keep those promises front and center, in front of our eyes. We have many different things vying for our attention so when we take the time to make a Christ-centered vision board and we put it in front of us each day, we are reaffirming our commitment to those goals and to taking the daily action steps we need to achieve those goals.

Vision boards can be in any format and be found anywhere. You can make a collage and keep it in your workspace, in your car, etc. But please, be mindful that your vision board is a personal piece and you don't need to let everyone see it. You do not need to let everyone see that because those are dreams, goals and desires that God has put on your heart. Now this can be challenging for people who do not live alone. As such, my suggestion would be to allow for the

Spirit to talk to you about where, how much and when you should be posting this so as to keep it private.

WHOA!

God will not usually give you dreams and goals that are easy to attain. They will be outside of your comfort zone, they will be out of your current reach and they will require His power to be accomplished. That is why this section is entitled: whoa! That may likely be your reaction when you find out what it is. As such, the right person God has for you may seem like a ludicrous idea to you. You may find out who he is and says "What?? Lord, You can't be serious!" I remember the first time I experienced someone in total disbelief over who the right man for her was. She was in total and complete disbelief and shared that she was not really attracted to him. She shared that she could never and would never think of him that way. Until one day she asked the Spirit to work in her to bring her together with him and the Lord changed her heart. He changed it so that she could realize that the friendship feelings she had had for him were really the solid basis for their romantic relationship.

Your Vision Board Will Likely Change

As we grow, as we move through life, please recognize that it is likely that what you choose (and what you are led to include) on your vision board is very likely to change. I recall wanting to work for a specific company that I felt would be a wonderful company to work for, until the Lord brought it to my attention that the reason He had brought that company to mind was because He wanted me to see why they were not the right company to work for. My vision board changed a few times over the months, sometimes becoming more specific and more detailed, sometimes including more images of those specifics, and sometimes making complete changes because I had grown in that respect.

I remember when I was looking to include a specific man on my vision board. He was (and is) very handsome, very cute and intelligent. I had him up on my board for weeks, praying for him and asking the Lord to being him to me. Until I realized that what I had asked for was completely outside of His will. He had brought the thought and name of this man for a completely different reason and purpose than I had thought. Instead of guiding me to be in a romantic relationship with the man, He had brought his name to me for the purposes of praying for him.

Make It Yours

Your board is meant to speak to you, to be a representation of what you feel led to and you should make it personal. Extremely so. Not only does making it personal help you to better connect with it but it also provides you with the opportunity to express yourself. We all need to express ourselves in a good, positive ways and this is one of the ways we have been given.

> Bear in mind that the Lord will never guide you to something that is contrary to His Word and His teachings.

But of course, bear in mind that the Lord will never guide you to something that is contrary to His Word and His teachings. In other words, God will never guide you to, for example, kill someone or take revenge on someone because that is completely contrary to His commandments and teachings.

Alyssa was feeling angry at her ex-boyfriend whom she found out had cheated on her multiple times. She wanted to include some revenge images on her vision board because she genuinely wanted to hurt him after what he had done. She felt that she had been very loyal to him and that his cheating ways were uncalled for. As time wore on, and Alyssa spent one on one time with the Lord, she began to realize that her approach had been wrong. She had been wrong to pray for her ex-boyfriend to be hurt because really simply, she needed to leave it all up to God. We are never supposed to take revenge or get even - we are supposed to leave that up to God who sees all and is able to do anything that needs to be done. In other words, God has ways of causing people to mature and to grow up so that they can be better people at the end of the day.

So, as her healing was taking place, Alyssa decided to leave her desire to get revenge on her ex to God. She had decided to release herself from that emotional burden and to let things happen as the Lord willed it.

Being Happy Is the Best Way to Live

When we are leading our best lives and we are happy, that is the best way to heal and to leave in the past those people and those situations that have hurt us in the past.

When we are happy, when we are feeling good, when we are taking care of ourselves mentally, physically, emotionally, we have to realize that that will come through in all ways. It will come through with cleaner and glowy skin, with greater happiness that radiates through our spirit, and we will feel at-ease in our bodies and at-peace in our minds.

Everyone at some point is going to feel hurt about something. That is inevitable but when we take care of ourselves and we are guided by the Spirit to do good and healthy things for ourselves, that is when we are working fruitfully on becoming the very best version of ourselves! Let God deal with those who do wrong and do bad!

It is never a good idea or recommended to take revenge on a person. That is not what we are called to do. We simply need to keep in mind that God is with us, sees all and that He will be the One to vindicate us. We do not need to take revenge into our own hands.

Praying For That Help

If you are feeling angry or hurt or depressed about how someone has treated you, ask God to heal you of those hurts, of those memories, of all that the person did to you. Ask the Lord to speak to your heart and to heal you of the hurt, the pain and the anger that you are feeling. Ask Him to help you feel better, even if the thing is still occurring. Here is a prayer that may help you in this area:

Lord Jesus, You have seen the pain, the hurt and the affliction I have endured at the hands of _____. You know all about the situation and You know what is really in that person's heart. I am asking You to come into my heart and to heal me as only you can. I am asking You to rid me of the hurt and the pain that this person or these people have caused and help me to move on to more abundant relationships. You are the One who is able to heal me and so I ask for You to do so. In Jesus' name. Amen

Remember that despite what some may be thinking, you are never bothering God by asking Him to come into your heart and to do something to help you. Remember that you are never asking for too much of His time to help in healing you. It is also a good idea to ask Him to bring to your mind any unfortunate memories you may have tuned out because of extreme pain, etc. If we leave those memories there, they will manifest in other ways which are not healthy so we want to rid ourselves of them by asking Him to help us be aware of them. Here is a suggested prayer for that:

Lord Jesus, You know all that I have been through. All that I have endured. I would like to ask You to bring to my mind any past hurts that I may have endured that I have forgotten about for the purposes of healing those wounds and helping me put that behind me. I do not wish for those past wounds to resurface in unhealthy ways so if there are wounds that I have forgotten about, please bring them to my awareness and heal me of them as only You can. In Jesus' name. Amen

Enjoy!

11

For Those Who Are Divorced or Husband(s) Deceased

If you are a woman who is divorced or your husband has died and you are now looking for your next steps, this chapter was written for you. Women who are not in that boat but are still curious about what happens here, this is good info for you too.

The first thing to say in this chapter is that if you are a woman who has lost her husband, I offer you my condolences.

I would also like to say that the Lord sees you, your pain, your past, your possible errors and loves you more than you know. Even if you have never known the Lord before, He knows you and He still loves you. Some women erroneously believe that because they are divorced that the Lord no longer loves them. That is not how God works. God loves you no matter what...that's what unconditional love is and He invites you into a loving, caring relationship with Him.

You know, it is literally never too late to come to God. Never. He welcomes relationship with you no matter where you've been or what you've done! You can consider this as your invitation to enter into a loving relationship with Him no matter what.

> It is literally never too late to come to God. Never.

The first step is to go to Him and to ask Him to come into your life. You can use this simple prayer to do that: *Jesus, I ask You to come into my life. You know where I have been and what I have done and I am asking You to come into my life in a real, meaningful and loving relationship with You. I ask You to show me the areas of my life where I need to repent and I ask You to activate the Holy Spirit inside of me so that I can have good guidance. I thank You in advance for answering my prayer. In Jesus' name. Amen*

There are many women reading this who have soured on marriage. They have possibly experienced marriage outside of what God intended for it to be and therefore they hold bad memories, there may be some reading this who had a wonderful marriage but their husband passed away from one thing or another, and there may still be women reading this who may feel a little angry with

God for allowing them to enter into a bad marriage or for taking away their husband in a way or earlier than they felt should have happened. To them, it is important to say that God knows and feels your pain and wants to have a close relationship with you so that you can experience the heart of a Father who loves you so much. He wants you to experience life with Him, even if you are currently angry with Him, even if you are currently confused by things that have happened, even if you are unsure of what your next steps need to be.

Put simply: the only way we are going to experience the goodness of what was meant for marriage is by experiencing it with the One who created it and this happens by letting Father God, Lord Jesus Christ and the Holy Spirit into your life. This does not have to happen with any pomp or ceremony - just a simple allowing of the triune Spirits to come into your life.

With the prompts of the Holy Spirit, you will be able to see how God can and will work in your life to bring about the kind of marriage that is loving, caring, mindful, present and stands the test of time.

You Were Never Meant To Do It Alone

You were never meant to do marriage on your own, no matter who you are. You were never meant to have to figure it out on your own, which I know is what some women reading this have done. We need to remember that we are not perfect and we will make mistakes, so will the man and so you both need to rely on the Holy Spirit's guidance and help to make it through.

I also want to make it clear here that when we go to the Holy Spirit for help, we are never shamed for doing so, nor will the Spirit ever make us feel bad or berate us. He will correct when something needs correcting but will do so in a loving way and one where you can understand what the next steps are and how you are supposed to handle the situation.

An example: Maya's fiance wanted to postpone their much-needed and much-deserved vacation so that they could both attend a conference he needed to go to for work. This conference was very important to her fiance's work and was mandatory for his job. He also made it clear that while he is sorry for having to postpone their vacation, that he was going to make it up to her with an even longer vacation and where they would go to at least 2 hot spots that he knew were meaningful to her. (Doesn't sound like a bad deal to me!) Maya was inflexible about the change of plans and she yelled at her fiance for even suggesting a change when, as she told him, "they both really needed this vacation." Maya's fiance was thrown. He couldn't understand why she was making such a big deal out of the postponed vacation and not seeing how he was trying to make the situation better. He was very disappointed. For days, Maya would not speak to him and would not even acknowledge his presence, saying out loud that she "doubted whether they should even go on any vacation or get married." Maya's fiance realized they were at a breaking point and prayed for the Holy Spirit to speak to Maya and calm her down while also getting her to come around for a conference she knew he had to attend.

The Spirit began to move within Maya and she slowly started to calm herself down. She realized that she had unfairly been yelling at her fiance and how wrong that was - a real recipe for ruining their future marriage (if they were to get there). Maya felt the need to pray and ask for insight and guidance. As the days wore on and the silence (and tension) between them seemed to have no end in sight, Maya's fiance made one final prayer for Maya to calm down because otherwise, as he said, he would have to take a break from everything that was going on and get some perspective on what to do next. Maya's fiance decided he needed to get some air and went out for a long drive. Because he was angry, he didn't see the stop sign at the end of the road and he experienced a head-on collision with a truck, which killed him instantly. Maya found out about this much later that day when the police officer came to her door to ask her if she knew the man by the name of her fiance and what her relationship to him had been.

Over the next months, Maya began realizing how unfair she had been to her fiance and how now, she would not have an opportunity to tell him that to his face. She prayed for how to handle that and the Lord reminded Maya that she can pray and ask her late fiance for forgiveness through God, by praying for God to forgive her and to let him know how sorry she was for the way she had been acting then.

Ladies, we will all make mistakes when it comes to our men and our relationships and so will our men, in one way or another. This is why we have Jesus there to help us through, to guide us, to "moderate" things if you will. We have to remember that we will sometimes need a minute of distance and that we need to tune-into what the Spirit is saying to us, even if at the moment it is a bit hard to hear.

"Sometimes I look at my husband and I just think..."

I remember being at a social event and a woman who was there said this line "sometimes I look at my husband and I just think..." and that sentence did not end well. We can have moments where we are human and we say or think things we don't mean. We can have moments where we are human and we really need to rely on the prompts of the Spirit to help us hold our tongues before we say something that we will regret later.

If you are getting to a point where you are thinking such things, it's time to take a good hard look at what is going on and while we are feeling that way. We are called to love our husbands and our husbands-to-be in a Godly way, as much as possible, and that will sometimes mean reflecting on what has been happening and how something can be fixed in as loving a way as possible.

Constructive Conversations

We have all heard of constructive criticism, now I present to you: constructive conversations. These are conversations we need to have with our man where we talk and discuss issues, concerns, worries and adjustments that may need to be made in the relationship. Every couple is going to have to compromise at some point in their relationship and when we do so after lovingly discussing and sharing our feelings and viewpoints, we can see how our compromise and our consideration to the other's feelings have really helped to strengthen the bonds of the relationship. After all, when we know that something is really bothering our mate, is it not incumbent upon us to discuss it with them and to find a reasonable solution? If you love your mate and you want to see them happy (which I assume all reading this do) you will happily make compromises, sacrifices and tailor everyday decisions so that both you and he are happy and satisfied in the relationship.

Constructive conversations, as a concept, are well in-line with the Biblical commands for a relationship: (1 Corinthians 13:4-8)

4 Love is patient, love is kind. It does not envy, it does not boast, it is not proud. 5 It does not dishonor others, it is not self-seeking, it is not easily angered, it keeps no record of wrongs. 6 Love does not delight in evil but rejoices with the truth. 7 It always protects, always trusts, always hopes, always perseveres.

In constructive conversations, nobody uses mean or defamatory words, unkind words or slanderous words. We are not here to do that. We are here to have a loving and calm conversation with our man so that they can feel heard, validated and that you are doing everything you can to make them feel happy and heard in the relationship. They should be working to make you feel the same way.

If you find the conversation heating up or not going in the right direction, there is nothing wrong with calling a momentary time-out (note that I did not say take a break because that denotes that you are technically broken up) and each does a different activity that will allow for some reflection time and space, away from the issues. This reflection time gives each party the space to move away and to get some perspective on the problem, allowing for greater and more constructive decision-making. It is also a good opportunity for both to reflect on whether the points you have made (and are maybe sticking to) are really that important to you. In every discussion, there are points that are particularly important to us, things that are very meaningful and that are "deal breakers" for us. Think carefully in this time-out whether the points you have made are just good to have or if they are, in fact, deal breakers. You will then be able to return to the conversation armed with a better perspective and better able to discuss what you really want.

It is never recommended to use any of the following in constructive conversations:

- Name calling
- Swearing
- Insulting of him or his family
- Berating
- Bringing up old hurts and issues
- Throwing anything
- Using sentences like "you always do this"

Even if the conversation is becoming a little bit heated, berating your man is never ok, nor is making him feel like less-than because he isn't right away doing what you want him to.

Asking the Holy Spirit to Rid You of Past Hurts

This was covered a bit further up but is so important that it bears repeating: we can sometimes continue to carry past hurts with us. Past hurts from previously unkind words spoken, from a divorce, from broken engagements, from having been cheated on and much more. Taking those hurts into your next relationship is almost inevitable unless we specifically work on asking the Holy Spirit to rid us of those past hurts. And He will. He will guide us to ways of ridding our hearts, minds and souls from past hurts in a way that no self-help book will be able to do!

Sometimes it can be as simple as a prayer to ask the Holy Spirit to do this. Here is one example of a suggested prayer you can use:

If you would like the Lord to bring to your attention old hurts that need to be healed because you may not remember clearly, you can use this prayer:

Lord Jesus, I ask You to come into my heart and to show me any past hurts that I may have forgotten about or that I may not realize. Please bring this hurt back to my recollection for the purposes of showing me how I can rid myself of the past hurt. Please show me step-by-step how I can do this. In Jesus' name. Amen

If you remember the old hurts that need to be healed, you can use this prayer:

Lord Jesus, I ask You to heal me of the hurt I experienced with _____ situation. I am asking You to help me heal from this so that I can move on from this in a healthy and happy way. In Jesus' name. Amen

Now, I invite you to take some time and write out your thoughts, feelings, impressions and anything else you would like to share. Remember, this is your own private healing journal entry and it is meant to be loving and helpful to you in every way.

Moving On From My Past??

For some women reading this, the mere idea of moving on past your old relationship or even your old marriage and looking forward to a possible new relationship and future marriage may seem impossible, even gut-wrenching. But it is possible that the Lord may be guiding you to a new chapter in your life - one that is filled with (more) happiness, laughter and beauty and that He may be trying to fill your life with but you aren't willing to let go of the past.

This is totally understandable but I encourage you to remember that God is perfect and sees things perfectly. If He is guiding you to move on from your past, whatever your past is, then maybe you could ask Him to talk to you about that.

Journaling is literally a two-way conversation between you and God (brought by literal words, feelings and sensations provided by the Holy Spirit). I'll say that again: literal words. He could be speaking to you or wanting to tell you something about your future right now. Are you listening? Are you willing to listen?

Asking the Holy Spirit to speak to you does not usually involve just asking Him once. Before I experienced this, I had asked the Spirit to speak to me many times, reminding Him that I was and am ready to listen, paper and pen-in-hand, ready to write everything down so I don't forget any of it and so that I record what I got accurately. Just as it was with me, He may not start speaking to you very clearly after one time of asking Him to - it may require asking again and again…and that's ok. Do so. He will because it is His will to speak to everyone.

Will you take the time now to ask Him to talk to you and to see what He would like to tell you? Write down anything you get here. Of course, if the space is not enough (and that would be great if it isn't), feel free to take more space (there are some pages provided at the end of this book for such a reason) or you can use a separate journal.

Do I Move On? What Does That Look Like...??

Now, for some reading this, you may have already been married and your husband or husbands have passed away. You may be feeling like getting re-married is not the right thing to do. While I do not pretend to know everyone's situation and life circumstances, I can suggest that you ask the One who does. Praying and asking God to reveal what His will for you is would be the wisest thing you can do. It is tremendously important to get His input and His take to see how He is leading you and guiding you in this area.

Another thing He can show you is what moving on looks like. Moving on is a general term and it can mean and look differently from one person to another, from one situation or circumstance to another. We have to be mindful enough to take our situation and all of its givens and ask God what He would have us do. He may guide you to heal and to be remarried, He may guide you to take years to heal from the loss of your spouse and to not get remarried. He is the One who knows how to guide you best and so consulting with the Holy Spirit is by far the smartest thing you can do!

 If you have lost your husband, please use this opportunity to ask the Lord and to pray over what you should do next. What are your next steps and what is He calling you to do? Remember that if you are new to journaling, take your time and remember that He does speak clearly to all who ask Him (and more times than not, we have to ask Him many times to begin speaking to us). He doesn't always respond after the first request.

_____
_____
_____
_____
_____
_____
_____
_____

12

Abuse

There will be women out there who are reading this who have been mentally, emotionally, intellectually or physically abused. To them, my utmost empathy. Abuse is horrible and should never happen. It is certainly not God's will for any person to ever be abused. God is a God of love and know that He sees you and wants to have an active and loving relationship with you, in case you didn't already know that.

Abuse is such a terrible thing and it does not come from God. There is no place for abuse in any kind of relationship, let alone a romantic one but man has free will and unfortunately, some men and some women choose to abuse their spouse or significant other.

> Remember, God loves you more than I can possibly explain and He wants to heal your hurts so that you can make your way over to the right loving relationship.

In this chapter, we will focus on you and your healing. Healing after abuse is necessary in order to move forward into a healthy, loving and wonderful relationship. Healing can begin to happen when we love ourselves and remember our worth.

Remember, God loves you more than I can possibly explain and He wants to heal your hurts so that you can make your way over to the right loving relationship.

Have you taken the time to build yourself up with loving, kind and caring self-soothing words? Have you taken the time lately highlight your wonderful qualities? Taking time out to do that is so important and it is important to consistently remind ourselves of our good qualities. We have to love ourselves and see ourselves as wonderful (just as God created us) so that we can be open and receptive to loving our God, ourselves, our man.

_____
_____
_____
_____
_____

_____
_____
_____
_____
_____
_____
_____
_____

I'd like to invite you now to remember that we have been made in the image of God. This means that we walk like Him, talk like Him, create like Him. Do you see yourself that way? If you do, great, give yourself a little pat on the back and encourage yourself to continue seeing yourself that way. If you don't, take some time right now and think about how you can get there. What are some things you can do right now and in the next few hours, and few days to get yourself to plant those seeds of good self-esteem inside of yourself?

_____
_____
_____
_____
_____
_____
_____
_____
_____

Healing Takes Some Time

I also want to take the time to say here that healing from abuse does not happen in 5 minutes. Healing is a process and that process begins with a self-love and remembering who you are as a beloved child of God because that is who He has created you to be. He loves you with an everlasting love and when you tap into that, your healing process goes much more quickly because you are working off of a solid base and foundation.

I also want to use this space here to say that positive words and affirmations will also go a long way. When you say positive words and affirmations over yourself, you begin tapping into the very thoughts God has and (had) over you. Our foundation and concept of self has to come from that because He is your Father, He is the One who made you and He knows exactly what He has put in you. When you tap into and begin to say and think those words over yourself, you are in essence getting into agreement with Him about who you are….and that is very powerful. When we remember who He created us to be, we think to ourselves "God loves me so much and created me like this and loves me with an everlasting love, just as I am." It is worth noting here that God does love you with an everlasting love. Whatever "imperfections" you think you possess, know that He loves you still just as you are. You wouldn't love your baby less if they were born without a limb….God is no different.

Yoga & Exercise

I also believe it is important here to encourage all women including those who have been through abuse of any kind, to get to exercise and do yoga with meditation. When we work on honing and toning our bodies, we are honoring ourselves, we are saying that we believe it is important to take care of our bodies and some ways to do that in a significant way are to:

- Exercise
- Do cardio
- Do yoga, while focusing on Christ and His love
- Engage in meditation
- Wear workout and yoga clothes that make you feel wonderful

The Clothes That Help You Feel Good

I recall very clearly and distinctly how terrible I felt in traditional, tight workout clothes when I was beginning my workout journey. The clothes I was wearing made me feel utterly terrible because I felt that they were accentuating the fat on my body. I felt better wearing loosely fitting clothes at the beginning because that was one way that I could feel better and like how I was looking while doing my exercises. It can be hard to get that motivation and when we wear clothes that don't make us feel good, well, that can influence us to work out less. I noticed how wearing clothes that covered me up a little more helped a lot when I first started.

Gradually, as I lost the weight, I felt more and more equipped and confident to wear clothes that were a little bit tighter and helped me feel more confident with my new figure.

You may be the same way but you may not but what's important is for you to get started because the mind-body-soul connection is very important in helping any woman feel like the best version of herself. It is really important to take care of all parts of ourselves so that we can feel whole, happy and good - which is the way God always intended for us to feel.

Self-Love Time: I want to take this time right now to give you an opportunity to reflect on your self love level. How are you feeling about yourself right now? Are you feeling good? Are you feeling sad? Take inventory of how you generally feel about yourself and ask yourself what you can do to help yourself feel better and feel more in-tune with your best self. Record your answers here:

_____
_____
_____
_____
_____
_____
_____
_____
_____
_____

_____
_____
_____
_____
_____

_____

Therapy & Counseling

Something I would like to say about therapy and counseling here for a moment. I believe strongly that therapy and counseling can be amazing tools for talking out problems, situations and helping one to heal. They can be amazing and there are many awesome therapists and counselors out there. I remember that when I was trying to deal with the abuse I suffered as a child, I needed to go talk to someone and get out my negative feelings about everything because it really simply was becoming something I couldn't get past on my own at the time. But I would like to suggest that if you are going to see a counselor, a therapist, a psychotherapist, etc., that you see one whose practices are rooted in Christian beliefs. The reason I say that is because you may want to work with someone who is knowledgeable and able to help you work through your issues, worries and concerns and who is firmly rooted in Biblical truth. There are other types of counselors out there and they may be using (most do) anti-Christian practices. I remember one that I was seeing for a little while that practiced a technique called "tapping". I didn't then and I still cannot understand how tapping would be helpful or how it was supposed to assist in healing me. Non-Christian-rooted counselors will use alternate practices than those from the Bible and that can definitely guide you away from an active and loving relationship with Christ.

13

Divorce

I will break this chapter down into 2 separate sections: those who are considering divorce and those who are already divorced. I include this information in a book about finding God's right person for you because you may need to be divorced for this to happen as your next step(s).

Those considering divorce are undoubtedly going through a hard time in their lives. Marital discord is very hard and it can really totally sap your energy. Also, if you are considering divorce, you may be feeling like God hates you. Please know that that is not the case.

Yes, God hates divorce but He also knows that sometimes, especially in cases where there is abuse, that divorce is needed. What are some important questions to consider (as honestly as possible) are the following:

- Have you done everything you feel the Spirit led you to do to salvage your marriage?
- Have you prayed about this?
- What is the Spirit telling you to do?
- Have you and your husband (separately and together) sought couples counseling?
- Have you spoken honestly and truthfully about the issues that you are (both) facing?
- Are you allowing yourself to be more influenced by your friends or family than you are by what God is guiding you to do?
- If the Spirit is convicting you (lovingly) about something you have done wrong or said something wrong, have you repented for that and gotten back on the right track?

Getting divorced or being divorced is not a good place to be but it does happen and we sometimes have to get ourselves out of a situation, especially if we are in danger or the Lord is guiding us to get out. People are not likely to know your situation intimately well because once we close the door, they don't see what we are going through. As such, we have to pray and take the problem to God. We have to ask Him if this is right for us, if this is the right time for it, if there is something He needs to bring to our attention that we have done incorrectly, and much more.

The bottom line is that God loves us way too much to leave us in an unhappy situation but He also loves us way too much to let us walk away from a good situation that may temporarily look bad or that is temporarily difficult. Every marriage is going to have its difficulties, that is not news, so we need to ask the Spirit about the degree, intensity, length, etc., that we are supposed to endure in a tough spot and whether enduring those things are in fact His will for us.

Joseph and Marina seemed like a happily married couple but behind closed doors, they were anything but. Joseph was hitting her and slamming her against walls. He would tell her that she frustrated him to no end due to the fact that she would go to see her mother without asking him. Joseph threw Maria against the wall so hard each time he did that the walls would shake. During one particularly heated argument, he hit her across the temple, causing her to temporarily lose a portion of her eyesight in one eye. Marina loved her husband so she suggested that they go to counseling. Joseph was not having any of it. He told her to go to counseling on her own. This would not be a marriage, with the givens unchanged, that God would want Marina to stay in. God would never condone that one of His children (and we are all meant to be His children) to stay in a situation like that.

Had the situation been different and Joseph agreed to go to counseling and to get to a place where he could be in a loving relationship,after having dealt with his anger issues, then Marina would very likely have stayed. When one partner is not willing to work to fix the issues and you see that for prolonged periods of time you are praying for them and looking for a positive and meaningful change but that things are not improving, then it is not likely that God will want you to stay in such a situation.

He Has Better For You

One piece of hope (at least, I pray that it does bring you hope) that I would like to present to people who are in difficult situations is this: if you do what you are supposed to do to support your mate and things are not changing, God will guide you to better. He will reward you for all that you have done to do the right thing.

Jade was in a similar situation to Maria. Her fiance had a drinking problem and Jade had gotten into praying deeply for him. She prayed for God to relieve her suffering by causing her fiance to realize that he needed help and to go to an AA meeting. For three years, Jade prayed for him, asking the Lord to encourage him to go to the meetings, to get help. Nothing was helping. She even did deliverance on him (the nature of which we will not get into in this book) but her fiance was not being receptive to anything she had been doing. Eventually, the Lord guided her away from this man He had once brought her. Jade was initially saddened and a bit devastated but she did understand why and she did not protest this. Several years later, Jade met and married Michael, a man whom God had guided her to, who loved her deeply and was a healthy person. Jade's desire was to have many children and this man was also able to give her that.

We need to make sure that we are doing the right things - we need to leave the rest up to God and be open to His prompts and His ways.

For those who are divorced, know that the Lord loves you and sees all that you have been through. There will be ladies from all walks of life reading this and the most important message is that God loves you and He wants to bless you.

When you have been divorced, you may have a sense of loss or of failure. Give that sense of loss or failure to God. You do not need to hold onto that emotional burden and the best advice I can suggest is to pray for what He has next for you. If you have made a mistake in your marriage, repent for your errors and then move on. You do not need to hold yourself in contempt for the rest of your life. God calls us to repent when we have made a mistake but never intended for us to keep beating ourselves up over the error or errors. (John 8:11) *"Go and sin no more"* is what Jesus said to the woman who had committed adultery. He had forgiven her and she was free to carry on with her life.

Anytime we sin (make any kind of mistake) we simply have to repent earnestly and then we are free to continue with our lives. God never meant for us to be forever condemned by our sin - we repent and we move on:

"I am the light of the world. Whoever follows Me will never walk in the darkness, but will have the light of life." (John 8:12) No matter what errors we have made, things we have said or done wrong, faux pas and more, if we go to God, admit our error and ask for forgiveness, He promises that He is just to forgive us. Take a look at the example of Suzanne:

Suzanne had made a mistake in her marriage to Stephen. She had had an affair that lasted a couple of years and it was eating her up inside. She made the decision to come clean to her husband, to admit the affair, to stop the affair, repent for it and then to accept the consequences of her actions. She knew that even if Stephen didn't forgive her, that God would. She came clean to Stephen and gently told him the truth. She explained how it had started, how long it went on and that she was truly sorry. She explained that she did not want to lead that kind of a life (one of lies and secrecy) and asked if he could, in time, forgive her. Stephen was devastated and said that he needed time to process everything. Of course, Suzanne understood that and she promised that she would do whatever it took to fix their marriage, for him to trust her again and for them to get back on track to the healthy marriage they used to have. Suzanne was doing everything she could to make things right. A year later, Stephen was no further along in forgiving Suzanne. When she calmly but firmly said that she was asking for his forgiveness and that she had ended things immediately with the other man, Stephen brushed her aside and said he had no time to deal with any of it. Suzanne began praying for Stephen's forgiveness and if it was the Lord's will, for their marriage to get back on track. A full year after that, things were no better and the Lord was now guiding Suzanne to move on.

> Despite her error and given her meaningful repentance and now-thoughtful actions, she still deserved love and the Lord was guiding her to another who would be able to provide that to her.

You Do Deserve Love

I want to point out a last (but very important) fact to end this chapter on divorce and that is this: despite whatever mistakes you have made, you still deserve love. God still loves you and that does not change. Ever.

I have heard of some people (men and women) who, because they have been divorced or are divorcing, because they are separated, because they sinned, because they have had an affair, etc., erroneously believe that they do not deserve love. Not so!

Harold was a sweet and kind man who was divorced. He had grown up his whole life believing that when you sin, God stops loving you so when his wife divorced him, he figured that God no longer loved him and so he stopped going to church. It took a very good friend of his over three years of consistent prayer for Harold to realize that God did, in fact, still love him and that he was welcome to go to church without shame.

> God loves you unconditionally yesterday, today, tomorrow and always. There is literally nothing you can do to earn more of His love. He loves you perfectly right now just as you are

God loves you unconditionally yesterday, today, tomorrow and always. There is literally nothing you can do to earn more of His love. He loves you perfectly right now just as you are and when He calls us to repent, it is because He loves us and wants the best for us and He can get that to us when we repent for any of our sins and mistakes.

Some may not know (or may need some help with) knowing the wording to repent for their sins. If you would like, you can use these suggested words for your prayer:

Lord Jesus, I know I have sinned. I have done _____ and I know that this is against Your commandments for the way that we are supposed to live our lives. I repent of my sins and I ask for Your forgiveness. I ask You to come into my heart and to heal me and to speak to me clearly so that I may begin to follow You in a healthy and loving way. I ask You to cleanse me of any other sins that I may not yet even be aware of. I ask You to come into my life and I'll make You my Lord and Savior. In Jesus' name. Amen

God will never turn down your honest and genuine repentance.

14

Firmly Committed

Please understand that when you are preparing for your loving marriage, you need to remember that loving marriage in God's definition is one where you, as a woman, are fully committed to your man in mind, body and soul and that Jesus is at the center of your marriage, there to support both of you. There are many versions of possible marriages, cohabiting situations, open relationships and more that are out there. Those are not God's ways or His recipes for a firmly committed and loving marriage.

(Genesis 2:18) *Then the Lord God said, "It is not good that the man should be alone; I will make him a helper fit for him."*

(Mark 10:6-9) *But from the beginning of creation, 'God made them male and female.' 'Therefore a man shall leave his father and mother and hold fast to his wife, and the two shall become one flesh.' So they are no* longer two but one flesh. What therefore God has joined together, let not man separate."

(Ephesians 5:33) *However, let each one of you love his wife as himself, and let the wife see that she respects her husband.*

When you are preparing for your loving marriage, as this book instructs and guides, understand that it means that you are firmly committed to the right man as the Spirit guides you. This means that you are firmly committed to understanding him, his values, things that are important to him, respecting and treating his family and his friends with the respect and dignity and kindness that they deserve, and being a real partner to him. It means that you are the person that he is going to need to go to and to bounce ideas off of and be supported by. We can sometimes have the misconception that men are independently strong and they don't need support from anybody. That could not be more untrue. As his partner, his wife, his fiancé, or his girlfriend, it is our role to be his support system and to be available to him, to talk to him through things, to pray with him, to give him perspective and to guide him closer to God and God's will for his life and your lives together.

I also want to point out here that we do not need to be his wife in order to be fully committed to him. As his girlfriend, or if you want to be his girlfriend, the onus and responsibility are still on you to be that helpful sounding board, that partner in prayer and in all matters. If we cannot bring ourselves to do that and instead we are directing our attention elsewhere such as by seeing other people, by engaging sexually with other people or in physical ways with other people, by not giving him our time and our attention, then we are not demonstrating that we are firmly committed to him and in fact we will have been less than honest because when you say you want to marry him, you are speaking of an exclusive and committed relationship with him and only him.

The world may have other ways in which they interpret relationships. That is not God's way. God intended for marriage to be that monogamous, committed, loving, supportive relationship and if you are not sure if you are ready for that or if you are not in the right headspace for that, you need to pray about that and to see how God is guiding you in that.

Sexually Adventurous

This topic is a major misconception about Christian marriages from both Christians and non-Christians alike. Many have the misconception that if you are in a Christian relationship, that sex, foreplay, teasing, flirting and sexual adventure are not for you. Totally untrue. God invented sex and He wants you to have it in plentiful and fun quantities and with meaningful quality with your husband. So explore, enjoy, dress up, role play, but do it all in a loving manner with your husband. Do it in ways where both husband and wife feel loved, cherished, honored and deeply respected. We can never experience better lovemaking than when we are feeling the most loved, cared for and respected by our committed, monogamous husband.

"Is It The Right Time?"

Sometimes, our hormones are calling to us, going nuts and we are wanting to get physical, including making love to, the man we are currently with.

Stop. Take your time. Get to know him as a person in a deep and meaningful way. Ask the Holy Spirit to help you make sure that this is the right man for you and then, after you are married and fully committed, enjoy the fruits of that union to its fullest extent.

During the dating phase, enjoy the many ways you can explore and be intimate with him. Kissing, for example, can be one of the most intimate acts we ever engage in. We are sharing a breath with that man.

I remember very clearly how a woman I will name Sandy was dating a new man whom she was extremely attracted to. She shared with me about her desire to sleep with him early on and how her body was calling out to her. When she went to go speak to her church pastor, she advised that while sleeping with this man might feel good, that it may very well cloud her judgment and that she needed to take the time to get to know him clearly for who he was. Oftentimes, we can let our judgment get clouded because of our physical feelings and hormones, not clearly taking into account that we need to keep our eyes and ears open in efforts to get to know the man. So, take your time, get to know him well and then, when you are sure and you are both firmly committed in marriage, enjoy making love as much as you would both like. God invented it so you can both enjoy it!

Domestic Duties

Cooking, baking, cleaning and tending house all fall under domestic duties and they are supposed to be done in partnership with your husband. Some of you reading this are already phenomenal at one or all of the duties mentioned and if that's you, good for you! If not, it's a great idea to begin learning how to cook, bake, tend to the house house and all of the pieces that come with that so that as a team, you can tackle those things together. (I refrain from calling them chores because they don't need to be simply "things we have to do" but rather, things we enjoy doing). Even if you and your husband enjoy eating out at times, having the skills of being a good or a great cook is one that will serve you both very well and knowing how to shop for the right groceries is so important. You need to be able to put together healthy, well-rounded meals that are also budget-friendly. I do a fair amount of the grocery shopping and some of the cooking and cleaning for my home and I tell you that it's a great sense of accomplishment and satisfaction when you know you have done a good thing for your family by knowing how to shop wisely and put together quick, colorful, healthy meals on a budget.

If that is not you yet, not to worry. It is never too late to get started and to learn how to be that domestically-awesome wife or woman.

Also falling into the category of domestic duties is cleaning. Again, if you do a little each step along the way, the home will remain a clean, organized and great space to be in. I know for myself that I had to be much more mindful in this area when I realized that my living space was not as neat and tidy as it should have been. I realized that I needed compartments, and that unlike others, I didn't like having shelves, but instead, that a standing clothes line was more suitable for me.

These things are all part of the preparation you will want to do to prepare for when you are married and there is another person relying on you or one with whom you are possibly sharing such chores as meal prep and weekly cleaning duties.

As women, we have many important responsibilities that we are blessed to be able to take on. Now, not every woman reading this will opt for every one of the responsibilities mentioned and I am not going to be one who tells you that you have to be the one to take everything on but picking and choosing the ones that are most meaningful to you and to your future with your family is important. Let's have a look and see the following list. Maybe you can jot a note or a little tick next to the roles that are meaningful to you and that you would like to begin prepping for for the future:

- Workout & fitness queen
- Great cook
- Amazing baker
- Wonderfully career-oriented lady
- Devoted mom
- Family caretaker
- Happy homemaker

- Neighborhood watch policewoman
- Prayer warrior

Who Will Benefit From Your Prepping? You Both Will.

How rewarding when you realize just how much awesomeness you do in your day and in preparing for your happy and healthy marriage. A woman I know was preparing to be a wife and a mom so she would visualize being in the car with her kids, taking them to soccer practice, ballet class, swimming lessons, Sunday school and also making time to take what she imagined were his parents to their doctor's appointments, baking for the school bake sale, learning a new language and more. She spent time each day visualizing herself doing these awesome tasks in her mind and in excited anticipation and preparation for the day when she would actually be undertaking these things. She would tell me how it felt to have her kids in the back seat of her car, eating their healthy after-school snacks and getting ready to go out on the playing field for their chosen sports and then she would get home in time to heat up the previously-prepared dinner she had made a few days earlier for the week and had popped into the freezer. This was a beautiful visual she had in her mind and she used that visual to co-create her reality with God. She knew it was also really important to her to have that wonderful relationship with her parents and with what she imagined would be his parents and so she would visualize herself making Sunday evening dinner with her mom and with his in the kitchen she dreamed she would have in the dream home she wished they would be living in. She spent time seeing this each day, visualizing each part of the image.

I'd like to give you an opportunity to develop your chosen visual and to see what items you would like to include in your visual. Think about all aspects of your home, your home life, your kids (if your vision includes kids), etc. This is an exercise where you are free to flex your inspiration and "wish" muscles. For example, there may be some ladies out there who are reading this and who may say "But Christine, I don't see how I will ever be a married woman or a mom" - set that aside for a moment and just allow yourself to be creative and to explore via your visual senses. See what you come up with and jot it all down here (all those beautiful, delicious details!):

_____
_____
_____
_____
_____
_____
_____
_____
_____
_____
_____
_____
_____
_____

That Conversation with Your Future Hubby

I think a book about preparing for a Godly marriage with your husband would be incomplete without talking about "that conversation" and what I mean by that is the conversation about how committed you will both be in this marriage, when it comes time to discussing that. Again, visualizing how that conversation might go whether you are with someone now or not is a great tool to use to prepare for how you would want that conversation to go and what that convo would look or sound like.

Discussing how committed you both will be and what that looks like in everyday terms is really important for you to both get onto the same page. I recall a couple I had heard about who had never had that conversation, so when I had spoken to the man who was now 5 years and two children into his marriage, he admitted that they had never actually had that conversation about what their commitment to one another (he and his wife) would look like. I recall that he expressed his actual shock that they hadn't taken the time to discuss that prior to getting married and that it was seemingly an obvious point but that no, they still needed to take the time to officially discuss it and say it out loud to each other.

Both husband and wife-to-be need to go into marriage with their eyes fully open and both being completely honest and forthright about what they want and what that would look like. People are not generally mind readers so we cannot expect either party to "just know" what the other person is thinking. We cannot expect either party to "just assume" that they know what the other person wants. Marriage is hard work and involves daily exercises in commitment, communication, love, compromise, fairness, consideration and more. Not only that but the way in which each performs these functions is also really important. I remember the case of Pablo who had met and married Maria, a woman he was nuts about but they had never discussed each of their roles before. Based on how their dating life had been, Maria expected Pablo to take care of everything for her and to not expect her to do too much since her main goals were fitness and looking great for him. Pablo's reasoning was that sure, it was great that she was so into those things when they were dating because she wanted to look really good for him but in their married lives, she would need to cook, clean and be domestic, including having at least two children which Pablo said were deal-breakers for him. That marriage was quickly dissolved when Maria realized his expectations and was not at all the kind of lifestyle she had in mind. She had set in her mind entirely different expectations and was not willing to meet and to compromise on those with Pablo.

Then, we can look at the example of Finola and Max. Finola was a career-driven woman when she had met Max but told him from the time of their second date that her intention was to take a big step back from her career to be a stay-at-home mom until such time as the kids were ready to go to school. She felt that this was also something God had wanted her to do since she had prayed over that in preparation for marriage. This was music to Max's ears since that was also exactly how he had seen things should be and he had appreciated how honest Finola had been about this.

In another contrast, Betty saw herself as a foster parent. She knew she was unable to have children and she was fine with that, and so she had told Randy that from the time they had started dating. Randy, on the other hand, felt it was very important for himself to be a biological father to his kids and while he was open to the idea of adopting or fostering children, he knew it was deeply important to him to be married to a woman who could make that a possibility for him. He did not therefore see Betty as the right person for himself and felt the Holy Spirit confirm that to him.

The example of Rowena is also really interesting. See, Rowena knew that she did not want to have kids but she was crazy about Ronald and she knew she really wanted to marry him. She had prayed about this and she knew that Ronald was the right person for her. Problem was that Ronald really did want kids and had expressed that to her so Rowena had a choice to make. If she wanted to marry Ronald, she would have to accept having their own children. Rowena made the decision that her desire to be with and marry Ronald was more important to her than any other desire, so she made the choice to marry Ronald and to accept having children with him.

Readers, when we discuss openly and honestly with your boyfriend, fiance, husband-to-be about our expectations and our ideals, we remove many of the pitfalls and problems that could arise later. This is all part of being firmly committed to having a great marriage and a great relationship. We cannot be firmly committed to the person without having had these "bottom line" conversations. Now, I recognize that it may not be easy to have these conversations or to know when is the right time to do so but I will say this: it is important to have them as soon as possible because if the mere topic makes your man or your potential man run for the hills, then this is probably not the right time or the right man for you. Yes, it can be hard to have those conversations but if we don't, we are setting ourselves up for a much grander disappointment down the line.

My last example here is of Whitney. Whitney sensed that her new boyfriend really enjoyed drinking, sometimes to the point where it was making her sick with worry because he would begin acting like a different person when he drank heavily. After some time dating, she was starting to see that this was getting between them and he was making a bit of a spectacle of himself at social gatherings. Whitney knew she had to have a conversation with her boyfriend to see what he was thinking and to see if, gently, he also acknowledged that there might be a problem here. He had expressed and confirmed to her that he knew that things were getting out of hand with his drinking but that he was unable to stop on his own. Whitney told him that she wanted to support him in making sure that he was healthy because she expressed that she did see a future with him. Her boyfriend was so touched and said he felt the same and that he wanted to enter a support program. Whitney told him that she would support him completely and so she stood by him for three years as he tried different programs until he felt he had found the right one. Whitney sacrificed a lot to support him in this endeavor because she had seen a future with him and felt the Spirit guiding her to continue supporting him for their future together. Whitney waited for him for three years while he was undergoing treatment, and even attended a support group for the friends and family members of those battling alcohol addiction. She knew that this man was the right person for her and so she had made the decision to stand by him as he was undergoing treatments. They were married one year after the conclusion of his fourth rehab stay, in an effort to give him all the time that he needed for a full recovery without feeling pressured to be "perfect" in the midst of his recovery.

So, in sum, being firmly committed is going to mean different things to different ladies reading this. It could mean that you know you are being called to sacrifice and to compromise, it could mean that you know you are being called to support your man and to be patient for him or it could mean that you are being called to help him or receive help on one or both of your journeys. Either way, being firmly committed is necessary if you are looking to get to the stage of a healthy, happy, firmly committed marriage.

15

Visualizing

It is really helpful to spend a significant amount of time allowing the Holy Spirit to show you what your future marriage is supposed to look like. Doing this while preparing for your loving Godly marriage is pretty important. Remember that your visuals are meant to be Holy Spirit-driven, so this is an important time (and point) to pray for the Holy Spirit to provide you with the right visuals. When He does, take the time to let the visual become really clear, to see all aspects of it, and to focus in on parts or areas you feel drawn to and led to.

Here are some Scripture passages to help you see how visualization was used in the Bible:

Habakkuk 2:2-3
Then the Lord answered me and said,
"Record the vision
And inscribe it on tablets,
That the one who reads it may run.

"For the vision is yet for the appointed time;
It hastens toward the goal and it will not fail.
Though it tarries, wait for it;
For it will certainly come, it will not delay.

John 1:51
And He said to him, "Truly, truly, I say to you, you will see the heavens opened and the angels of God ascending and descending on the Son of Man."

Genesis 15:1
After these things the word of the Lord came to Abram in a vision, saying,
"Do not fear, Abram,
I am a shield to you;
Your reward shall be very great."

Matthew 26:26-28
26 *While they were eating, Jesus took bread, and when he had given thanks, he broke it and gave it to his disciples, saying, "Take and eat; this is my body."*
27 *Then he took a cup, and when he had given thanks, he gave it to them, saying, "Drink from it, all of you.* **28** *This is my blood of the[a] covenant, which is poured out for many for the forgiveness of sins.*

Psalm 23

The LORD is my shepherd, I shall not be in want. He restores my soul. He guides me in paths of righteousness for his name's sake. Even though I walk through the valley of the shadow of death, I will fear no evil, for you are with me; your rod and your staff, they comfort me.

Hebrews 12:1-2

12 Therefore, since we are surrounded by such a great cloud of witnesses, let us throw off everything that hinders and the sin that so easily entangles. And let us run with perseverance the race marked out for us, 2 fixing our eyes on Jesus, the pioneer and perfecter of faith. For the joy set before him he endured the cross, scorning its shame, and sat down at the right hand of the throne of God.

Isaiah 1:18

Come now, let us reason together, says the Lord: though your sins are like scarlet, they shall be as white as snow; though they are red like crimson, they shall become like wool.

Proverbs 29

When the wicked rule, the people mourn—The righteous consider the cause of the poor—A fool speaks all that is in his mind—Where there is no vision, the people perish. 1 He, that being often reproved hardeneth his neck, shall suddenly be destroyed, and that without remedy.

We can see clearly from these passages that visuals and visualization are not only important, they are vital for the advancement of life. If we fail to use the power of visualization, we will be lacking the tools that God is guiding us to use to perform and to complete the work that He has guided us to do. As such, "the people" (you in this case, will "perish") and what I mean by that is not literally to perish but to not fulfill all that you have been called to be blessed with.

Here is a prayer to get you started with this: *Holy Spirit, I ask You to come and show me clearly a visual that represents my future marriage. I am looking for and seeking lots of details from you, which I plan to use to help guide me along my path to my husband and to a happy, healthy, fulfilling relationship with him. I ask You to speak to me clearly about this and to help me see, feel and acknowledge all that I need to. In Jesus' name. Amen*

Use this space to write down any and all details you get about the visual, including feelings and sensations you get during your time of seeing your visual. Remember that God speaks to us through feelings and sensations as well so when you do get those, pay close attention to them:

_____
_____
_____
_____
_____
_____
_____
_____

Again & Again

One cannot visualize once and then consider the job done forever. It doesn't usually work that way. We have to be consistently seeing the thing in the eyes of our heart and in our mind's eye. We need to be tuned-in and aware of this so that we can engage in this practice again and again. Here is a visual that I believe is really important in this section on visualizing:

In her hand, the little girl has a little teddy bear, which she loves. Jesus is kneeling down (coming down to her level) to let her know that He has something even better for her behind His back. When we look closely to analyze this picture, not only do we see Jesus leaning down to come down to her level in love, consideration and respect, but we also see Him dressed in white robes (indicating angelic trust) and He has His hand outstretched toward her in a loving and non-threatening way, allowing for her to see that He wants to give something to her, not take something away. We see how pleasant, kind, warm and welcoming the face of Jesus is, as we can see He is almost smiling at her. We can also see the huge teddy bear that He has behind His back and that He is indicating that He wants to give her, which is about 10 times the size of the teddy bear she is holding.

> Jesus is always willing to meet us exactly where we are and to begin an active, close and loving relationship with us from exactly where we find ourselves.

I really love this image because Jesus is coming to her, facing her, coming down to her level, making her a great offer. He does this for all of us...He meets us where we are. If you are hurting, Jesus will take you from there. If you are unsure, Jesus will take you from there. If you are needing help, Jesus will take you from there. He is always willing to meet us exactly where we are and to begin an active, close and loving relationship with us from exactly where we find ourselves.

A Picture Really Is Worth A Thousand Words

Why did Jesus use visuals to communicate with us? Why does He still?

Because He knew that 1) we have been created as visual humans and 2) because He knew that visuals were and are a way to communicate significant amounts of information in a shorter amount of time.

So, when Jesus shows you a picture of your future that He wants to bring you, He is looking to communicate a lot of important information fairly soon so that you can understand His ideas and His intentions toward you.

Asking The Holy Spirit To Explain The Visual

Many people ask me if it is acceptable to ask the Holy Spirit to explain a visual to us. It is not only acceptable, it is recommended. The Holy Spirit is always looking to communicate God's will to us, to help us, to guide us and to assist us in any ways that we need. He is looking to make the picture and the explanations as crystal clear as possible and as such, and in an effort to best understand the fullness of the image, we can definitely ask questions and probe the picture.

As an example, say you were provided with the following image of your wedding day:

We cannot see the man in the image but we get some clues as to some of his likely qualities. My point here is that God will give you an image like this (as He gave me) and you will need to probe, look carefully, examine and ask about the factors in the picture. Sometimes also the picture God gives you might be a little bit fuzzy. You will need to ask for details.

I recall the very first time the Lord gave me an image of my wedding day. I was in a white dress on a dance floor, dancing with my new husband and I had an idea of his size, hair color, style of hair and more but what I wasn't aware of was who he was, where I was going to meet him, when, etc. That came months later when I prayed about this and He led me to a certain location at a certain time where I would meet the man who would be the one He was guiding me to.

Wants To....Not Guaranteed

Now here is an important point: A visual is a reality God wants to bring us. It doesn't mean it's a guarantee that the visual will come to reality and to fruition. Why? Not because God is cruel or He wants to keep something good from us but because there are actions, steps and choices that need to be taken on the part of both man and woman involved for the visual to come to fruition. You (as the woman) can do all that you need to do to make this happen but if the man does not do what he needs to, then the vision will not come to be. Conversely, he can do all that he needs to but if you as the woman don't do what you are supposed to, then again, the visual will not come to fruition.

I will use the example of Joanna here. Joanna was a lovely young woman who really wanted to meet and marry the right man for her. She did receive many visions, all involving her husband-to-be and all involving going to what she saw in the visions as a BBQ that she would need to attend to meet him. She was waiting for the invite for that bbq because she felt that that was where she would be meeting him. An invitation for a bbq came a few weeks later from a friend of hers and sure enough, she did attend. She met Adam. He was sweet, charming, well-educated, professional, kind and most importantly, he was very kind and respectful toward Joanna. Joanna had shared about her visions received with her friend who was the hostess of the party and she used the opportunity to let her friend know that this was the man she believed was in her vision. Joanna and Adam had a great time chatting at the BBQ and when he was about to leave, he did not ask for Joanna's number. She was a bit disappointed but she thought that he might ask their mutual friend (the one who threw the BBQ) to pass Joanna's number to him. No such request came. Joanna was perplexed. She knew that they had had a connection and he seemed to find Joanna lovely, engaging and intelligent.

The factor that was missing in that case was that Adam was not a man of faith and so he wasn't praying to God for his wife in the same way that Joanna had been. Joanna then began praying for the Lord to reveal Himself to Joanna and to make a move - something he chose to do a bit later.

That's the unfortunate thing that happens when both parties are not following God - they can miss out on the greatest of blessings because they were not aware or tuned-in to the steps needed to make it happen.

Here is the example of Maya and Rick. Both were praying people and while Rick was looking for his future wife and had been praying for that and had received a vision about it, Maya had not. She had not yet met Rick but had not decided that she even wanted to be married - she was quite fulfilled and content with her career. So Rick began praying for God to cause the right woman to cross his path. It was a few weeks later that he met Maya and knew instantly that she was the one for him. As he got to chatting with her, he realized that Maya was uncertain about wanting to be married, so he began praying fervently that if that was indeed God's will, that He would cause Maya to be sure that she wanted to get married. He prayed for months for this and it was only when he felt he was being guided by the Holy Spirit to do so, did he ask Maya out on a date.

She agreed to go out with him and they had a fantastic time. During their date, Rick shared about his vision and that he had been praying for Maya to decide whether she wanted to follow God's will and be married. Maya had said that she sensed that the Lord was guiding her in that way and so she had made the choice to get married. She had shared that her apprehension came from not wanting to give up her successful career as a lawyer, to which Rick promised (in one of those courageous conversations) that he would not want her to give up her career and that he could and would support her in that endeavor for as long as she and the Lord wanted her in that career. We can clearly see here that both man and woman made the decision to follow God and to do His will for His desire for both of them.

Aligned With God

When we get on the same page as God regarding our lives, we come into complete alignment with His will for our lives. We begin to put in place all the steps that we need to and that are required to come into alignment with His will for our lives. He knows His best plans for us and He knows how to get us there.

Many people make the assumption that God's will for their lives is going to take them away from what they want. I want to take this opportunity to tell you that in all likelihood, the desires you have in your heart have been put there by God so He is going to be guiding you to His best way to accomplish those desires.

I cannot overstate the importance of feeling the happy feelings and tapping into those feelings when He provides you with a vision.

What if His will is different from your desires? Then I would suggest putting down your will and following His. He is God and He knows best, sees all and always has your best interests at heart. When He gives you a vision, try to tap into the feelings and the joy from experiencing those realities, even in vision format. If you are having some trouble with this, ask the Holy Spirit to help you with it. I cannot overstate the importance of feeling the happy feelings and tapping into those positive feelings when He provides you with a vision and as usual, the Spirit is there to assist you with this.

Taking a moment to tap into this: Let's take a moment to tap into a vision He may want to bring you right now and to check-into the happy feelings of such a vision. Allow yourself to experience these and to fully be open to all parts of the vision. Remember to:

- see and explore all aspects of the vision
- ask questions about what you are seeing
- ask for clarifications on what you are seeing
- note any sensations you get from seeing the image
- do you notice anything about timing?
- do you notice anything about seasons?
- what are you wearing?
- tap into the feelings of seeing yourself in that space
- allow yourself to be fully open to this and remember that you may not see a way of fulfilling the vision but He has ways.

_____

_____

_____

16

That First Date

The first date.

Such an exciting time for you and for him. Planning where you will go, how he will pick you up, what you will wear, how you will do your hair....such fun things to think about.

When we get ready for our first date with this awesome man, we want to put our best look on by wearing our favorite outfit that helps make us feel most confident, do our hair in a way that allows us to toss it in a flirtatious manner and do our makeup with flawless execution. Most importantly, it's really important to just be ourselves.

Sometimes on a first date, we can get so nervous about how we will look, what we will say, etc., and the most important thing to remember with that is ensuring that we are being our natural and beautiful selves. Show him the real you by being the happy, beautiful, confident woman that you know you are. He is going to be looking to see how you dress, how you hold yourself, how you speak over yourself, to him, possibly the wait staff at the place you are going. All of these things will tell him so much about you and all the good qualities of yourself that you want him to know about.

Of course, you will also be checking him out: what he wears, does he drive, does he hold the door open for you, how respectfully he treats you, how much pre-planning has he put into this date, how he speaks and much more. This is your fun opportunity to get to know him and to let him get to know the awesome lady you are.

Dressing Well

When you're going out on a date, it is really important to dress nicely but not like you're going into a business meeting or the beach (unless your first date literally is going to the beach). A lovely outfit that matches the season with fashionable pieces that highlight your favorite features would be great and showing a little skin in a tasteful way is a nice idea too. Great shoes with a bit of a heel are also usually a great idea, as is some jewelry.

Hair & Makeup

It's really important for your hair to be clean and well-styled. It's also very attractive when we have hair that is tousled (whether long or short) and shows our fun side. Again, this is not a business meeting so there is no need to put up your hair as though you are going into a business meeting.

For your makeup, accentuate and highlight your best features with minimal makeup that makes you feel good. Wear makeup that is durable no matter the temperature because you don't want, say, your non-waterproof eyeliner running down your face or your foundation coming off during one of your activities.

Treating Him Right

As much as you will be looking to see how he treats you during the date, it is also really important to realize that he will be looking at how you treat him. You want to be sweet and kind and your awesome self…after all, he chose to come on the date and he found you attractive enough to ask (or in the case of a blind date, he agreed to go out with you) or in the case of your having asked him, he agreed to go out with you.

Treating him right implies taking a real interest in his life, his friends, his family, his work, his dreams, his aspirations, and any other things he chooses to share with you. Asking him questions is not only ok, it is recommended. Remember that you are trying to figure out if you want to see him again or not. Have fun with the date and with him. You are supposed to enjoy spending time together. :)

No Games

Dating your future husband should never be about playing games. In other words, if you are interested in seeing him again, tell him so. You don't need a "3 day wait rule" to see if you want to proceed with him. Let him know and tell him that if he is interested, you'd be happy to see him again. If you need some time to think about whether you would like to see him again then you can let him know that you had a great time and that he is welcome to call you again if he would like to. It should not be about playing games by making it seem like you're not into him until you know that he's into you.

A date with your future God-given spouse is supposed to be about getting to know him, showing him who you are, and not about playing games.

Appreciating His Gestures

When a man pays for you during a date, it is customary and polite to say thanks for everything. Some women I have seen believe "he is even lucky I agreed to go out with him, of course he's going to pay for me". I'm not sure this is the right attitude. Perhaps instead, you can be grateful and show some appreciation for his gestures - after all, he is trying to show you a nice time and to get to know you. If you don't appreciate his gestures from the first date and express those to him, that will reflect poorly on you.

Sending him a thank you and appreciation text at the end of your date after he has left and letting him know you had a great time is a really classy move. Whether you both move forward together or separately, you will both look back on this one day and he will recall how you treated him and you will recall how he treated you. You both want to remember the other as kind and giving.

If It Doesn't Go Well

You can be on a date with the man God has guided you to but maybe...it won't go well. I have seen this happen to some wonderful ladies. If this happens (and it does happen), please pray over this. What I have found to usually be the case here is that if this happens, it is because one party is not very close to God and so they may not be feeling the same thing as the other. It would be wise to pray to see how God can help to ensure that things move forward in the right way and in the right timing (as in, not yours or my timing, but His).

17

Now You Are Married....Now What?

All your preparation. All your hard work. Now you are married. Congratulations!

Now what do you do?

Well, for one thing, you enjoy the fruits of your marriage and the fruits of having taken the time to prepare for this special time. You have put in place the conversations, the expectations, the feelings, the skills, the habits and much more...

This is the time now to trust that you have done your homework correctly and it is time to enjoy this married time with your new husband. It really is such a special time and if you are fortunate enough to have loved ones who are supporting your marriage with good thoughts, prayers and well-wishes, then you are increasing your likelihood of staying happily married.

You see, this book was intended to be a homework piece (if you will) about how to set the foundations right in your marriage. Once you have set those and you are now married, it is time to lean on those foundational pieces and have the conversations, undertake the prayers and much more that you will need to lean on for the rest of your future.

Remember that your marriage was intended to include Jesus so when (not if) you find that you need strength, help, perspective, reasoning, understanding, support, the right words and more throughout your years together, **go to Jesus and ask Him to help and to support**.

There may be times when things don't go so "fairy tale" such as a possible time of mistrust, strife, difficulty, misunderstanding or other such bumps in the road. It can be easy to fall into the routine of life and to stop communicating as much with your spouse but this is why we need to put in place regular "relationship check-ins". This means that to keep the relationship fresh, we have to keep all of the following in-place:

- Regular individual and couple church and prayer times
- Regular date nights
- Praying together each night
- Hugging and kissing every day
- Sharing our feelings about things without holding back
- Regularly praising one another
- Regularly forgiving one another when that is needed
- Talking through problems, issues, ideas

- Talking through next steps
- Being and remaining kind and respectful to each others' side of the family
- Remaining supportive of each others' career and career needs
- Always speaking well of each other (and never putting the other person down, especially in front of other people)
- Praying for each other when the other is going through some difficulties
- Going out of your way to support one another and really being there for the person
- If you have kids, not letting the kids take over your lives but rather, always finding time for each other
- Always doing sweet and unexpected things for one another
- Asking God for strength and understanding when things get difficult

All About Maintenance

If you have guessed that a healthy and happy marriage is all about maintenance, then you are correct. It is. And maintenance needs to be done regularly and with love. I cannot stress enough that criticisms, put-downs, insults or other have no place in a healthy and happy marriage and it is so important to make sure that this is being practiced by both man and wife.

When we realize that we have made a mistake with our spouse and a comment, an idea, a suggestion, a mean-spirited thing was said, we need to stop and apologize immediately. Once we get to the point where we are continuing to lead our daily lives and just sweeping the problem under the rug, we are allowing the enemy to seep in and to systematically begin destroying the fabric of our relationship. Not talking things out and not being honest are recipes for total disaster.

I remember watching an episode of Workin' Moms and the wife and the husband were in bed, discussing something. They seemed like a happy couple from the outside but it turned out that each of the husband and the wife were actually having affairs and had not told the other. They clearly had some issues that had not been talked about and so they were both going outside of their marriage to satisfy something that was missing. That is never ok nor is it the answer. The affair is a manifestation of something bigger that is lacking in the relationship and that needs to be figured out and discussed. We have to be honest with our husbands (since this book was written for ladies) or our fiances or our boyfriends because the issues that don't get tabled and resolved will result in such unfortunate things happening.

Have You Thanked God?

When you finally do get married, please remember to thank God and to acknowledge Him in all ways. He is the One who orchestrated the two of you coming together and He is the One who created you both for each other. I hope you will remember to thank Him both privately and publicly.

It would also be a wonderful opportunity for you and your new husband to set aside some time each week to reflect on God's goodness of having brought you two together. You can reflect together for years to come on this - remember that keeping in mind for years to come that He brought you both this blessing is also a great way to remember just how much of a blessing it is, even during the tough times.

18

Some Final Thoughts

I want to take this opportunity to congratulate you not only for finishing this book but also for completing the exercises within its pages. Following through on the work means you are taking the steps necessary and needed for a loving, amazing, fulfilling, Christ-centered marriage. It is not easy to reflect so honestly and to work on yourself but it is time very well spent. You will be really happy that you put in place all of the good things on your side, giving you and your future husband the highest chances for a very healthy and happy marriage.

This is one of the greatest and most significant decisions you will ever take. As such, it would be wise to complete these steps and even to share them with your church group, pastor, etc.

I want to encourage you to start or to continue to lean on the Holy Spirit for help and for guidance with anything. Whether it is 2 am or 2 pm, the Spirit is always going to be there, helping you and guiding you to your best life and your best lives together.

Be open to the promptings of the Spirit because He does not operate in a manner meant to hurt you or to accuse you but rather, to help you see where you have gone right and where you have gone wrong. We all need to gain perspective and sometimes, as well-meaning as they may be, our friends and family may not be able to either be available or they will not have the benefit of the same 360 degree view that the Holy Spirit will be able to provide you with.

When we say "I do" at the altar, we are saying yes literally to all of the following:

In the name of God, I, _____, take you, _____, to be my wife/husband, to have and to hold from this day forward, for better, for worse, for richer, for poorer, in sickness and in health, to love and to cherish, until parted by death. This is my solemn vow.

This is meant to be a firm commitment that we are making to love this man firmly, and as unconditionally as possible. He will make mistakes, you will make mistakes and it is really important to recognize that you both need to love and cherish each other through those mistakes.

I want to encourage you, reader, to work on yourself until such time as that happens. Again, not because there is something wrong with you but because we are all works in progress. We are all trying to do our best and one of the best ways to do our best is to start from a place of self-love and self-appreciation. Note that I did not say to be puffed up with pride. Nope. Self-love and pride do not have anything to do with each other. When we love ourselves, we do our best each day but we also forgive ourselves when we don't do things the right way. Just as there will be times in your future marriage where you will have to make the choice to accept when your husband (and later, possibly, your kids for those who don't already have kids) did not do something the right way or the way you wanted it done and you will have to accept that he is not perfect.

Working on our self love is a process and it takes some time. Some reading this will be further along on the continuum while others may be just at the beginning. That's ok and it's great. What matters is that you started and how much effort and time you put into it.

Imagine yourself 3, 4, 5 months from now having done the self-love exercises, stated your positive words of affirmation, done the actions required for a healthier mind, body and soul and ensuring that you have kept the right people in your life - just imagine how much further along you will be! How much more in love with yourself you will be!

Such an important point: when we learn to treat ourselves right, we keep around us and we teach others to also treat us right. We do not need people who will put us down, use negative words, be unkind, etc.

I will never forget how a woman I used to work with would consistently put me down. She would mock everything about me, putting me down at every chance she got. I knew why she was doing this and life took me away from her anyway but it taught me something about how some people can be: when they feel threatened by you in any way, some will lash out in this way. It's not your problem. It's theirs.

When we lean on and we remember Jesus' love for us and how He died on the cross at Calvary for us, we remember that we are to die for! The King of Kings died for us. There is no greater or grander deed. There is no greater love than that. So on the days (or the hours) when you may be feeling less than excellent, please remember that. He loves you and He believes in you so much that He laid His life down for you. Think about that for a moment. Let that really marinate in your mind just what that means.

I may never meet you, dear reader, but I want to convey how lovely I think you are. Internally and externally...just lovely. God made you the way you are and as such, you are His wonderful creation. He made you in His image, which means we walk like Him, we talk like Him, we create like Him and so we need to remember our place and our responsibilities unto ourselves and unto others. We have a responsibility as creators to create wonderful, awe-inspiring things, from personal relationships to professional endeavours. The following examples are of relationships, works, professions and careers that women may be engaged in. I use these to show that women in general can and should love themselves, their future husbands, their future children and if God calls them to, to be wonderful creators in the professional space He has called you to.

As a woman, create a love for yourself and for the people around you.
As a woman, create a deep(er) relationship with the Lord, Father God and with the Holy Spirit.

As a woman, create a wonderful home for you and your loved ones.

As a surgeon, create a very successful (possibly life-saving) surgery.

As a teacher, create a wonderful environment and incredible lessons for your students.

As a painter, create great works of art that speak to the heart of those who see it.

As a dentist, create excellent smiles and more that help people feel really good about themselves.

As a writer, create wonderful works that when people read your work, they are transported to another place of hope and of love.

As a hairdresser, create beautiful hairstyles with an array of colors at your disposal that allow others to express themselves and to feel good about how they look.

As a furniture designer, create comfortable and ergonomic furniture pieces that people will simply be thrilled to have in their homes, offices, and spaces.

As a bus driver, create a smooth and pleasant ride so that people can get to where they want and need to go.

As a stay-at-home mom, create a space where your kids are engaged, can learn and can grow into the awesome human beings God created them to be.

As a chef, create culinary delights that are both visually appealing and deliciously scrumptious.

As a lawyer, create an argument for your clients that will influence the judge to vote in your favor.

I think you get the idea. Thank you for reading my book. I pray that it not only helps you tremendously but that if you feel so inclined, that you pass it on to a female friend, family member, colleague or acquaintance so that they too can benefit from these words and from a closer relationship with Christ.

Notes

Please feel free to use this for additional notes and space for jot notes, ideas, prayers, journaling, etc.

www.ingramcontent.com/pod-product-compliance
Lightning Source LLC
Chambersburg PA
CBHW050348120526
44590CB00015B/1605